P9-DGH-035

THE QUILT DIGEST

THE QUILT DIGEST

THE QUILT DIGEST PRESS
SAN FRANCISCO
4

© The Quilt Digest Press 1986. All rights reserved.
ISBN 0-913327-06-9
ISSN 0740-4093
Library of Congress Catalog Card Number: 82-90743

Edited by Michael M. Kile.
Book design by Patricia Koren in association with Jeanne Jambu and Laura Smith,
Kajun Graphics, San Francisco.
Editing assistance provided by Harold Nadel, San Francisco.
Typographical composition in Sabon by Rock & Jones, Oakland, California.
Color photographs not specifically credited were taken by Sharon Risedorph
with the assistance of Lynn Kellner, San Francisco.
Printed on 100 lb. Satin Kinfuji and 260g/m² Bon Ivory (cover) by
Nissha Printing Company, Ltd., Kyoto, Japan.
Color separations by the printer.
First printing supervision by Roderick Kiracofe.

On the cover is a detail from "The Dream," a painting by David Bates.
See page 68 for a complete photograph of this work.

Second printing.

The Quilt Digest Press
955 Fourteenth Street
San Francisco 94114

CONTENTS

❧

Pine Tree Quilts
by Suellen Meyer

The origins and development of one of America's most revered
patterns are discussed in this pioneering presentation.

❧

"Helping the Peoples to Help Themselves"
by Nancy Callahan

The Freedom Quilting Bee of Alabama, a black, self-help
co-operative of women, is introduced.

❧

Showcase
Compiled by Roderick Kiracofe

Twenty-four antique and contemporary quilts are shared
in this fourth annual display of beautiful quilts.

❧

Old Maid, New Woman
by Shelly Zegart

Accompanied by the "Old Maid" quilt her friends made for her,
this is the true story of a nineteenth-century single woman
and her life of dedicated service to others.

❧

Quilts in Art
by Penny McMorris

The influence of quilts on contemporary art is aptly
illustrated by the works of several artists.

❧

The Collector: On the Road
by Michael Kile

Never-before-published quilts from a quilt dealer's private collection
are shared, along with her thoughts about collecting.

PINE  TREE

Made by Mrs. Madray, Pulaski, Tennessee, c. 1880–1910, 91 × 72½ inches, pieced cottons. Collection of Bets Ramsey.

QUILTS

PINE TREE QUILTS, like the trees which gave them their name, appear across the United States, from Maine to Florida and from the Atlantic Ocean to the Pacific. From the earliest days of white settlement, the pine caught the American imagination.

In fact, without the pine, settlement might have been delayed. When Captain John Smith and his men sailed from England for Virginia in December 1606, they planned to find, not pine trees, but gold. Captain Smith wrote in his *Generall Historie of Virginia* that there was "no talke, no hope, nor worke, but dig gold, wash gold, refine gold, load gold."[1] Unfortunately, the adventurers found no gold and faced the prospect of being recalled to England when they could not repay their debts to the Virginia Company, which wanted quick profits.

In desperation, they looked for something valuable, and they found the pines. Working furiously, they downed trees, cut them into clapboards and wainscoting, tapped trunks for turpentine and pitch, burned trees for potash and collected resin for waterproofing the ships.[2]

The Company would have preferred gold, but the king was delighted. England had been buying lumber and masts for her ships from the Baltic lands; now she could get them from her own colony. Soon the king's emissaries arrived to mark every white pine over two feet in diameter with a broad arrow to reserve it for the Royal Navy. Special ships carried as many as fifty hundred-foot masts back to England. By the nineteenth century, American white pines were supplying half of Europe's needs as well as building America's boats and houses.

Although the forests offered great economic gain to the harvesters, they frightened most; they also varied widely. In Massachusetts, the forest resembled a park; some tree trunks remained branchless for the first twenty or thirty feet. More northern forests presented a tangled mass of overgrown trees, vine-clad and dense. In the Maine wilderness grew spruce trees twenty feet around and others so large no ship could carry them.[3] The face of the forest mattered less than its implacable, unknowable presence.

American women, both the seventeenth-century British immigrants and later the pioneers, did not like the wilderness. In it lived Indians who, according to all accounts, would kidnap them and their children. Wild animals yowled and threatened. Their husbands, hunting or exploring, often left home, sometimes for weeks at a time, expecting women to deal with the Indians, the animals and the weather on their own. Rather than wringing their hands and fainting, as did the heroines in romantic novels, they faced their fear and set about domesticating nature.

The dense wilderness induced claustrophobia in the newcomers. Anne Bradstreet said that when she came to America in 1630 her "heart rose" against the country. Joan White, who lived for some time near Salem, Massachusetts, never got used to the country, complaining of being "shut up for a long space of time living far in the woods."[4] As women moved west, they echoed this refrain of the earliest settlers. Grandmother Brown reported in her memoirs, when she moved to Iowa, "My heart sank.

SUELLEN MEYER

'Don't let's unpack our goods,' I said to Dan'l. 'It looks so wild here. Let's go home.'" They stayed, but she was not happy there.[5]

As the land became domesticated, women forgot their fears. By the late 1700's, land near the towns in the original colonies resembled the cleared, ordered, domestic landscape the earliest colonists had yearned for. Many women living on the eastern seaboard, on plantations or in sophisticated seaports like Charleston and Baltimore, had the time and inclination to make beautiful quilts. Still impressed by the culture of England, they turned there for artistic direction and found the gentle, romantic *Tree of Life.*

Unlike the American view, which wanted to dominate nature, the eighteenth-century British aesthetic glorified nature and delighted in its exuberance.

English gentlemen, bored with the formal geometric gardens of their ancestors, created new "natural" pleasure grounds. They emphasized meandering streams, winding paths and informal groupings of trees. Into these grounds, landowners introduced the occasional hermit, paid to be unkempt, solitary and visible—but not *too* visible--accompanied by cows, sheep, deer and peacocks. The hermit and animals, though carefully scripted, suggested the innocent harmony of nature and provided guests with topics to while away their time at picnics. After dining, they were led to view a particularly pleasing "prospect," usually a stand of fine trees.

In fuel-hungry England, people revered trees because the demand for wood for heating, cooking and shipbuilding had denuded the countryside. Huge trees and forests became the mark of wealth.

Thus, gentlemen set aside parkland for their peers and the ladies to admire. Admire it they did. Elizabeth Bennet in *Pride and Prejudice,* for example, falls in love with Mr. Darcy only when she sees his park. This appreciation of romantic landscapes led Englishwomen to create elaborate cloth ones.

For beds and windows, artists designed crewel hangings that emphasized trees, flowers and animals. Soon British factors sent these same designs to their agents in India, who ordered Indian printed and painted cloths in similar designs. Thus was born the British form of the Indian *palampore,* which was soon translated into the fashion of the day for bedrooms. The American populace which identified itself with England wanted the same fashionable hangings. Everyone who could afford them ordered them. Others imitated *palampores* by cutting chintz and appliquéing their own. Thus, the earliest known American tree quilts,[6] made by women of wealth and refinement, bore the signs of upper-class British attitudes toward nature.

Rural women, unlike the British nobility or wealthy American city dwellers, depended directly upon the land, the sun and the rain for their food, their shelter, their livelihood. Because of this dependence, they were particularly responsive to nature.

In their journals and letters, nineteenth-century rural American women frequently described their surroundings, often emphasizing the trees they saw.

Detail from " 'Allisonia' Property of C. H. Allison Esq.," from Illustrated Atlas Map of Cooper County, Missouri, *1877. Photograph courtesy of Missouri Historical Society, St. Louis.*

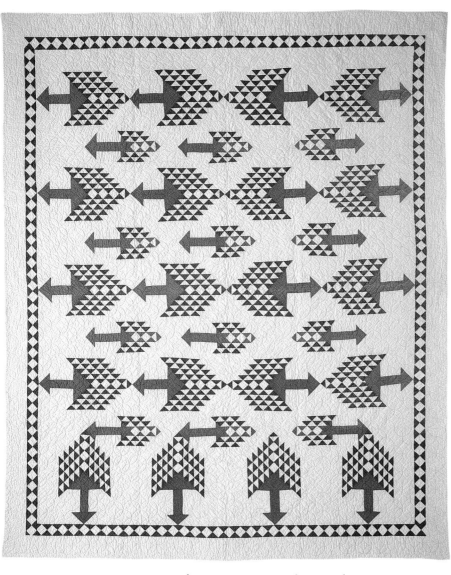

*c. 1860–1875, origin unknown, 77 × 92 ½ inches, pieced cottons.
Collection of Tonia Sledd.*

America's first landscape artist, A. J. Downing, approved of shade trees but urged his readers also to plant evergreens, especially hemlock and white pine, for "they are the body guards ... which properly defend the house and grounds from the cold winds, and the driving storms, that sweep pitilessly over unprotected places."[8]

Women understood Downing's view. They knew that gardens and trees turned houses into homes, streets into neighborhoods. They planted joyfully, ordered seeds and saplings from the many nurseries that sprang up in the nineteenth century and traded prized specimens with one another.

When women, usually at the behest of their husbands, turned to the West, they carried few possessions but a lifetime of memories. For many, trees—especially the sheltering evergreens—signified home. Their letters and diaries abound with references to the new scenery, often noting the flora that reminded them of home. Narcissa Whitman, a missionary moving to Oregon in 1836, recorded in her journal the flowers, berries and trees she saw, noting "a beautiful cluster of pitch and spruce pine trees, but no white pine like that I have been accustomed to see at home."[9] For another Oregon pioneer, Amelia Stewart Knight, the trees were awe-inspiring: "Many of the trees are 300 feet high and so dense to almost exclude the light of heaven, and for my own part I dare not look to the top of them for fear of breaking my neck."[10]

Interest in the landscape helped pioneer women endure hardship. Although their wagon was mired in the mud west of Kansas City, Miriam Davis Colt consoled herself by enjoying the flowering crab apples:

Meanwhile, we women folks and the children must sit quietly in the wagon to keep out of the rain—lunch on soda biscuit, look at the deep black mud in which our wagon is set, and inhale the sweet odor that comes from the blossoms of whiteness along the roadside.[11]

When Sarah Francis Hicks, who deliberated for eight years before marrying the slave-owning Dr. Benjamin Wilson in 1853, moved from her home in New York to his plantation in North Carolina, she found things to dislike but took solace in her surroundings. She wrote to her parents, "The woods present a beautiful appearance now, the rainbow hues of autumn contrasting beautifully with the deep dark green of the pines. Many of the trees are hung with vines of the honeysuckle, woodbine and others."[7]

As the country matured, farms turned into villages, villages into towns, towns into cities. Residents, feeling rooted and safe, laid out parks, planted shade trees in their yards and lined their streets with sugar maples and American elms.

Naturally, such sensitivity to nature could work against a woman's happiness as well. A Mormon woman, writing about the unending journey through the plains, confided, "We have come 1500 miles in wagons and a thousand miles through the sage brush, and I'd get into the wagon tomorrow and travel a thousand miles farther to see shade trees instead of these rocks and sands."[12]

Few pioneers coming from the settled areas of the East could imagine the wilderness and isolation of the frontier. Inevitably, the dreams of some travelers were shattered by its reality. Anna Shaw long remembered her mother's first view of the log home her father had prepared in the Michigan frontier:

I shall never forget the look my mother turned upon the place. Without a word she crossed its threshold, and standing very still, looked slowly around her. Then something within her seemed to give way, and she sank upon the ground....When she finally took it in she buried her face in her hands, and in that way she sat for hours without moving or speaking.... Never before had we seen our mother give way to despair.[13]

Anna Shaw's mother, like other women, stayed and endured. They did not allow themselves to recognize their deprivations—not, that is, until something struck them. Mrs. Hilton, a pioneer in the Kansas prairies, asked to accompany her husband when he announced he was going to Little River for wood: "She hadn't seen a tree for two years, and when they arrived at Little River she put her arms around a tree and hugged it until she was hysterical."[14]

For many women, the tree symbolized the comfort of home and the intimacy of domesticated lands. Early in their housekeeping, pioneers turned to cultivating their gardens and planning their landscaping, duplicating when possible their memories of home. Eliza Farnham's sister Mary spoke for many women when she said, "I have often thought if I were placed in a world where nothing but exquisite loveliness and forms of beauty grew around me, I should still crave some familiar object, however plain; something

which I had known in the old home; something which would be a visible link to the bygone."[15] For her, the familiar objects were flowers and trees. Describing her lawn, she said, "Every tree and shrub which we planted in our grounds was a companion, whose growth it was delightful to watch."[16]

Mary Colby, creating a home in California, clearly recognized the value of familiar trees in curing homesickness, for in 1849 she wrote to her brother and sister in Massachusetts, "When our fruit trees begin to bear it seems more like home   we have apples pear peaches and plum trees."[17]

Many women mentioned their fruit trees, perhaps because they depended upon the fruit for preserves and for drying, or perhaps because it suggested home and family. From Missouri, Sophie Duston wrote to her father in New York that she had planted apple and plum trees.[18] In Iowa, Sarah Carr Lacey and her children transplanted wild plum and crab trees from the river bank to her orchard. While she was about it, she cut slips from willows and poplars and planted them in her yard.[19]

c. 1870-1900, found in Greensville, New York, 73 × 70 inches, pieced and appliquéd cottons. Collection of Darwin Bearley.

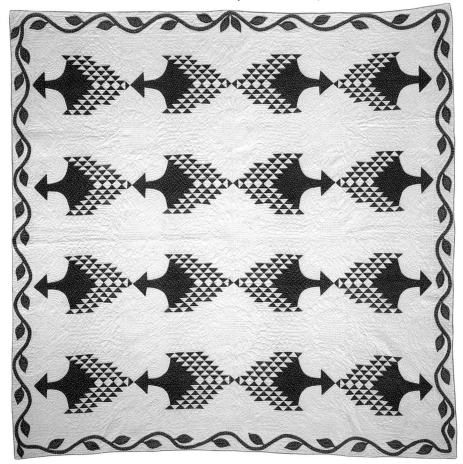

At least one woman had the foresight to take her trees with her on the journey west. Miriam Davis Colt noted, "Our wagon is heavily loaded...eight trunks, one valise, three carpet bags, a box of soda crackers, 200 lbs. flour, 100 lbs. corn meal, a few lbs. of sugar, rice, dried apple, one washtub of little trees, utensils for cooking, and two provision boxes—say nothing of mother, a good fat sister, self, and two children."[20] Once Miriam reached Kansas, she was ready to set out her trees and re-create home.

Trees signified home to many people. After a couple built a new house, they usually planted a tree to mark its completion, so that, across the country, houses and the trees in their lawns date from the same period.[21] In New England, the tradition was to plant "husband and wife trees" on each side of the entrance or on the east side of the house.[22] In Illinois, Eliza Farnham noted that a house was not finished until the trees had been planted: "The little cottage in which they were to find their future home was completed and entered. Trees were set about it, outbuildings constructed, and the farm began to wear a cheerful and inviting look."[23]

Even when the tree was cut down, its stump was a reminder of the house it had graced. Mary Rabb recalled the 1833 flood of the Colorado River:

We stayed in the house until the water was over the floor. Me and some of the little ones had to be carried to the wagon as the water was over a foot and half deep in the yard. We had to hurry to get out to the hills. Your pa and a Frenchman by the name of Bateas hurried back to try to save our goods, our beds, and clothing. They got to the house and pulled the things up in a cedar tree that was in the yard, not right in front of the house, to one side. The cedar tree is cut down, but when I go a fishing, I visit that old stump and the place where the house used to be.[24]

Trees marked houses not only for their owners but for others as well. In the prairies, where settlers could see for miles, trees indicated neighbors and community. Mary Blankenship, who settled with her husband in the midst of cattle country in Texas, remembered the comfort of trees: "The neighbors' places were beginning to show up in the shimmering mirage of distance, as their trees began to tower above the new homes."[25]

Whether in one's own yard or in the yards of neighbors, trees were intimately associated with domesticity, family and comfort. For many women,

trees spoke of home. Their mothers and sisters tended the gardens, planned the planting and shared horticultural lore. Transplanted women recognized the trees of home and tried to live with them. Trees were so important emotionally that, where they did not grow naturally, women improvised. One woman, sick of sagebrush and yearning for a fruit tree, set up a small willow branch outside her cabin door and decked it with artificial flowers to "make blooms on the little tree."[26] Such an emotional reliance on trees made them a natural design for quilts.

Indeed, many kinds of trees turned up on quilts. First, of course, were the elaborate *Tree of Life* quilts inspired by the British. Some other early nineteenth-century quiltmakers appliquéd cherry trees. Maple, laurel and oak leaves emblazoned some quilts, and others were quilted in leaf designs. But, far and away, the most popular tree design was the pine.

From the time of the earliest settlers, the pine had been the symbol of the New World. Because New England white pines grew to 250 feet, they towered over all other trees in the forests. They were extremely valuable, providing fuel, turpentine, resin, tar, paints, lampblack, tanbark and pitch. The pine dominated the settlers' imaginations. The first coin minted in America, the Massachusetts Bay Colony shilling, featured the pine. The pine also appeared on early flags: the Bunker Hill flag, the Continental flag, the Vermont flag and the Massachusetts naval flag.

The settlers' *pine* included more than pines: it was a general name for hemlock, fir, spruce and cypress. The French traveler Chastellux described the new Americans' language:

Anything that had no English name has here been given only a simple designation: the jay is the blue bird, the cardinal the red bird; every water bird is simply a duck, from the teal to the wood duck, and to the large black duck which we do not have in Europe. They call them "red ducks," "black ducks," "wood ducks." It is the same with respect to their trees: the pine, the cypresses, the firs, are all included under the general name of "pine trees."[27]

Since the settlers came from a land bearing fewer than one hundred varieties of forest trees to one with almost one thousand, a great deal of renaming was necessary. Even though the settlers and later the pioneers might refer to many different trees as *pines,* they were very clear about what each species offered. The shipbuilder used white oak for the timbers of ships, cedars for exposed areas, pitch pine

for pitch and turpentine, and white pine for masts.[28] Women's use of wood was generally more domestic, encompassing vital everyday tasks.

Maintaining fires usually occupied many hours of a woman's fourteen-hour workday. Her first morning task was to build up the fire; her last evening task was to bank it. In between, she brought in wood, built up the fires for cooking or warmth, and checked the wood supply. If the fire died out, she had to go to a neighbor for a burning ember to start it again. Martha Ballard, aged sixty-nine, took care of her wood herself, though she did not enjoy it. "I broke old loggs with an old hough, and brot in the pieces in a basket; and how fatagued I was."[29]

Cooking with wood was no easy task, since each species has its own idiosyncrasies. Women had to recognize the wood, know how long it had been cured and adjust their cooking. Even when they could afford cooking stoves rather than fireplaces for cooking, they needed skill. One recipe for biscuits emphasized the difficulty:

Stoke the stove, get out flour, stoke the stove, wash hands, mix biscuit dough, stoke the stove, wash hands, cut biscuit dough, stoke the stove, wash hands, put biscuits in oven, keep on stoking until the bread is baked and ready for table.[30]

Trees also provided the means for one of the housewife's chief occupations: keeping her family and her surroundings clean. Women scrubbed with lye soap made from wood ashes, boiled the wash water over wood fires, swept the floors with brooms made from hickory branches. Other women used bowls, spoons and utensils carved from wood, rigged beds with hickory staves and entertained children with wooden toys. Even ink came from oak galls, hardened blisters on oak trees.

Whether living on farms, in villages or in cities, women cared about trees. In settled areas, they

Prior to receiving the patent to her land, this California homesteader had already set out trees on her property. Photograph courtesy of the California Historical Society/Ticor Title Insurance (Los Angeles).

13

Detail from a quilt made by Mary Haynes Boothe,
Washington County, Tennessee, c. 1890–1910, pieced cottons.
Collection of the author.

separated trees into ornamentals (like the pine) and food-bearers. Women living comfortably in a town or city might see the duality of the fruit trees, which combine beauty and practicality, but consider others, like the pine, as merely ornamental. Rural women would see both qualities. Women everywhere, town and farm, East and West, recognized the abiding emotional content of trees. Like Downing, they knew the pines guarded the home both physically and psychologically. Surrounded by trees, they could withstand winter winds and loneliness. The pines presented a perfect subject for quiltmakers.

THE *PINE TREE*'s origin is shrouded in the past. Ruth Finley, in *Old Patchwork Quilts,* asserts that it is a colonial design, originating in Massachusetts but made in each of the original thirteen colonies.[31] While it is fashionable to consider researchers like Finley as romantic amateurs, it is quite possible that the information she reported is factual but the supporting evidence has been lost. Although women wrote about quiltmaking in their letters and jour-

nals, they did not always describe in detail the designs they were piecing. This information would, however, be shared orally: women would know which designs were popular where and when. For *Old Patchwork Quilts,* published in 1929, Finley might have interviewed women born in the mid-1800's. They, in turn, might have repeated information learned from their mothers born in the early 1800's. In other words, what modern critics term "wishful thinking" might well be the truth passed through an oral tradition which did not survive two world wars and massive migration.[32]

Thus, it is possible that the *Pine Tree* does date from colonial days. If so, it sprang from the generation which, revering pine trees, stamped them on shillings and appliquéd them on flags. An enterprising seamstress might well have transferred the tree design from the flag to a quilt. If so, she probably appliquéd the image on the quilt rather than making it a part of a pieced design.

It is more likely, however, that the pattern dates from a later period. No geometric *Pine Tree* has been authoritatively dated to the eighteenth century. However, in the second half of the nineteenth century, they were made throughout the country. Many date from the 1860's to the 1890's, a time when the country was recovering from the Civil War and when thousands of pioneers were heading westward. As Americans searched for stability, the pines might have reminded them of what they had survived and might have given them hope for the future. Sewing the pine, a national image of stability and rootedness, into a quilt, a visible manifestation of home and domesticity, the quiltmaker could acknowledge her roots and family even if she had moved far away.

The *Pine Tree* design itself cuts through elaboration in order to focus on essentials. It is, therefore, very different from the eighteenth-century *Tree of Life* quilts. Like the English pleasure grounds which inspired them, these appliquéd *Tree of Life* designs encouraged variation and emphasized the individuality of each tree. Even though some quiltmakers began with the same textiles, they ended with very different scenes, each more exotic than the previous one. The geometric *Pine Tree,* on the other hand, reflects a different aesthetic. This design demands precision in the cutting and piecing and emphasizes essentials. It strips the tree of identifying characteristics so that only trunk, branches and leaves

c. 1890–1910, Tuscaloosa County, Alabama, 71 × 79 inches, pieced cottons. Collection of Robert T. and Helen Cargo.

15

remain. This reductionist approach to design, typical of folk art, allows the *Pine Tree* to stand for all trees. The name, far more than the design, evokes the vast pine forests still in the American consciousness in the nineteenth century. Without that name, the design might imply an oak or maple, an apple or pear.

The design must have struck a deep chord in the quiltmakers who used it, for, though the tree block lends itself to startlingly creative arrangements in which the tree disappears, almost all makers organized the trees in rows, setting the blocks on their points (page 6). This organization isolates each tree, emphasizing its separateness. Frequently, the quiltmaker set rows with the points of the trees facing to the center of the quilt so that, when it is placed on a bed, the trees appear right side up from either side, like rows of trees lining a drive or walk (pages 10 and 11). Other variations occurred. Some quiltmakers, setting their blocks on point, separated the rows of trees with streak-of-lightning stripping. Others split the trees edging the border, so that half-trees appear in every other row. But most adhered to the rigid organization of whole trees in parallel rows.

A number of quiltmakers maintained the essence of the design while personalizing it. Mary Haynes Boothe, of Jonesboro, Tennessee, uncovered the earth around the tree trunks to highlight their roots. These tiny triangles show the depth of the trees and hint at the rootedness and safety they represent (page 14). An anonymous Alabama quiltmaker set the blocks on the square rather than on the point so that the trees appear to bend in the wind—but not to break (page 15). A third quiltmaker placed her tree solidly in the center of the quilt, encircling it with many borders (page 17). Though these variations may be seen as fairly simple in themselves, the resulting quilts feel delightfully idiosyncratic and very personal.

Eventually, of course, some quiltmakers designed bold arrangements in which the individual trees disappear. Perhaps these quiltmakers had more time or money for experimentation, but equally likely, they were freed from the fear of the forests which permeated both the early settlers and the pioneers who had to deal with the raw land. Whatever the cause, rare and exciting variations exist. In one, attributed to Hattie A. Zehner of Pennsylvania, the quiltmaker presents the pines as a huge star, their foliage sections connected, their trunks radiating outward (page 18). This star variation was popular in the long-settled countryside of eastern Pennsylvania after the Civil War. In this variation, the trees are subordinated to the overall design. Perhaps the awareness of the emotional importance of individual trees encouraged most other quiltmakers to treat them independently rather than as part of a whole.

Throughout most of the nineteenth century, the *Pine Tree*'s design and name remained basically intact, with a few quiltmakers adding personal variations. By the end of the century, however, quiltmakers were clearly playing with both the design and the name. The *Ladies Art Catalog* for 1897–1898 showed both the traditional *Pine Tree* design and variations of it, each with a different name. The 1897 *Orange Judd Farmer* shows it as *Weeping Willows*, while a late-1890's *Hearth and Home* calls it *Centennial Tree*, a thoroughly appropriate name considering how important the pine was to American settlement.[33]

Once design variations began, the *Pine Tree* collected other names as quiltmakers combined the enduring image with new enthusiasms. Ohioans, in the throes of Prohibition fever, renamed it *Temperance Tree*. The Women's Christian Temperance Union, founded in Ohio, campaigned tirelessly for temperance; early supporters urged abstinence not only from alcohol but also from "strong drinks" like tea and coffee. Oberlin Professor George Whipple warned that quiltings could be injurious to health, for they provided "a source of great joyousness and there was also some extraordinary eating and drinking." In fact, he reported that at one quilting an excited young lady went into convulsions and died—a direct result of "drinking strong tea rapidly."[34] The name *Temperance Tree*, like the Eighteenth Amendment itself, quickly lost its popularity.

Most of the new names clustered around religious beliefs. By the 1930's, some were calling the *Pine Tree* the *Tree of Paradise*, the *Tree of Life*, and even the *Tree of Temptation*. All refer to the Tree of the Knowledge of Good and Evil and to the Tree of Life in the Garden of Eden. Although not identified by species in the Old Testament, the Trees of Knowledge and of Life are clearly fruit trees, which the pine is clearly not. However, by the twentieth century, the direct connection between the pine's image and its name no longer mattered. As the wilderness it had represented was domesticated, the pine could absorb other important emotional content; for some, that content was religious.

For others, it was secular. Some quiltmakers, keeping the traditional design of triangles for leaves, called their trees *Apple Tree* or *Patch Blossom.* Others changed even the leaves, substituting squares for the triangles and renaming the design *Cherry Tree* or *Little Beech Tree.* Still others improvised, using diamonds (*Lozenge Tree* and *Live Oak Tree*) or little cones for foliage (*Cone Tree,* referring to a nut-bearing pine).[35]

Like the American version of English, which learned to give names to every variation, the *Pine Tree* gathered names for each change in emotion as well as in design.

THE *PINE TREE* quilt's change in design and name reflected the change in women's consciousness. From the 1600's until the end of the frontier, men equated the New World with the Garden of Eden. In 1630, just off the *Arbella,* John Winthrop wrote from Massachusetts, "We are heer in a Paradice."[36] Two hundred years later and three thousand miles farther west, J. M. Shively promoted California by evoking the magical fertility of Eden: the "plains produce an abundance of oats and clover spontaneously."[37]

Unlike these male popularizers, women refused to see the wilderness as Eden and worked assiduously to create from it their own version of the Garden. As they hewed homes[38] from the great forests, they honored the image of the pine, a symbol both of the chaos they feared and of the domesticity they intended to create. When they looked about their homes and saw that they, not the wilderness, had survived, they felt freed psychologically. Then they could manipulate the cloth image just as they had the reality; they,

not nature, massed the trees, creating from them a new reality.

The new environment included gas and electricity, modern replacements for the wood which had undergirded civilization. By the Depression, almost eighty-five per cent of women in villages and cities used electricity; soon rural women benefiting from the Rural Electrification Administration followed suit. No longer did rural women need to check the woodpile or stoke the stove. They, too, learned to see the pine as ornamental.[39]

The struggle was over: women had won their gardens from the grip of the wilderness. The pine tree became emblematic of other issues. Still, underneath the new pattern names lay the power of the pine and the reverence for the land which once boasted white pine trees taller than a twenty-story building. The origin of the *Pine Tree* may be lost, but its emotional significance remains in hundreds of letters, diaries and journals of nineteenth-century women alive to their surroundings and eager to recount them.

c. 1880–1900, Pennsylvania, 77 × 78 inches, pieced cottons.
Collection of Mary Strickler's Quilt Collection.

Made by Hattie A. Zehner, Snyders, Pennsylvania, c. 1890–1910, 79 × 80½ inches, pieced cottons.
Collection of Marvin C. Rogers, the quiltmaker's grandson.
Submitted by the Vermont Quilt Festival, Northfield, Vermont.

18

REFERENCE LIST

1. Richard B. Morris and the editors of *Life, The New World: Prehistory to 1774* (New York: Time Incorporated, 1963), p. 50.

2. C. William Harrison, *Forests* (New York: Julian Messner, 1969), p. 72.

3. John R. Stilgoe, *Common Landscape of America, 1580 to 1845* (New Haven: Yale University Press, 1982), p. 26.

4. Annette Kolodny, *The Land Before Her: Fantasy and Experience of the American Frontiers, 1630-1860* (Chapel Hill: The University of North Carolina Press, 1984), p. 7.

5. *Grandmother Brown's Hundred Years,* quoted in Norton Juster, *So Sweet to Labor: Rural Women Working on the Land* (New York: The Viking Press, 1979), p. 169.

6. For photographs and a full discussion of *Tree of Life* quilts found in Charleston, South Carolina, please see Lacy Folmar Bullard, "Once Out of Time," *The Quilt Digest 3,* pp. 8-21.

7. Joan M. Jensen, ed., *With These Hands: Women Working on the Land* (Old Westbury, N.Y.: The Feminist Press, 1981), p. 84.

8. *Rural Essays,* ed. by George William Curtis (New York: Leavitt & Allen, 1857), pp. 327-328.

9. Reprinted in Leon Stein, ed., *Fragments of Autobiography* (New York: Arno Press, 1974), p. 54.

10. Diary reprinted in Lillian Schlissel, *Women's Diaries of the Westward Journey* (New York: Schocken Books, 1982), p. 214.

11. Cathy Luchetti and Carol Olwell, *Women of the West* (St. George, Utah: Antelope Island Press, 1982), p. 81.

12. Elizabeth Wood Kane, *Twelve Mormon Homes* (Tanner Trust Fund, University of Utah Library, 1974), p. 86. Quoted in Sandi Fox, *Quilts in Utah: A Reflection of the Western Experience* (Salt Lake City: Salt Lake Art Center, 1981), p. 7.

13. Sandra L. Myers, *Westering Women and the Frontier Experience 1800-1915* (Albuquerque: University of New Mexico Press, 1982), p. 141.

14. Mary Furgusson Darrah, quoted in Joanna L. Stratton, *Pioneer Women: Voices from the Kansas Frontier* (New York: Simon and Schuster, 1981), p. 80.

15. Eliza W. Farnham, *Life in Prairie Land* (New York: Harper and Brothers, 1846. Reprint by Arno Press, 1972, American Women: Images and Reality series), p. 247.

16. Farnham, p. 243.

17. Schlissel, p. 157.

18. Letter from Sophie Duston, Petitsaw Bluff, Missouri, to Hugh White, Utica, New York, 24 January 1825, in *Missouri History Papers,* Missouri Historical Society, St. Louis.

19. Glenda Riley, *Frontierswoman: The Iowa Experience* (Ames: The Iowa State University Press, 1981), p. 59.

20. Luchetti and Olwell, p. 81.

21. Stilgoe, p. 165.

22. Eric Sloane, *A Reverence for Wood* (New York: Dodd, Mead and Company, 1965), pp. 47-48.

23. Farnham, p. 213.

24. Jo Ella Powell Exley, ed., *Texas Tears and Texas Sunshine: Voices of Frontier Women* (College Station: Texas A & M University Press, 1985), p. 171.

25. Exley, p. 252.

26. Myers, p. 145.

27. William Cronon, *Changes in the Land: Indians, Colonists, and the Ecology of New England* (New York: Hill and Wang, 1983), p. 8.

28. Cronon, p. 109.

29. June Sprigg, *Domestick Beings* (New York: Alfred A. Knopf, 1984), p. 43.

30. Riley, p. 62.

31. (Philadelphia: J. B. Lippincott Company, 1929), p. 100.

32. I am indebted to Cuesta Benberry for this interpretation of Finley.

33. Communication from Cuesta Benberry.

34. *The Graham Journal of Health and Longevity,* 8 June 1839, p. 194, quoted in *Quilts and Carousels: Folk Art in the Firelands* (Exhibition catalogue, Firelands Association for the Visual Arts, 1 May to 4 July 1983), p. 28.

35. Barbara Brackman, *An Encyclopedia of Pieced Quilt Patterns,* Vol. 2 (Lawrence, Kansas, 1979), pp. 82-87.

36. Kolodny, p. 6.

37. Kolodny, p. 233.

38. Women did indeed "hew" their homes from wood. While few women actually built their homes themselves, they did work with the men in cutting off the smaller branches from the trees and dragging the timber to the wagons or homesite.

39. Susan Strasser, *Never Done: A History of American Housework* (New York: Pantheon Books, 1982), pp. 81-82.

SUELLEN MEYER is a quilt writer, lecturer and historian, as well as Assistant Professor of English at St. Louis Community College-Meramec. In 1982, she received a grant from the American Association of University Women to study Missouri-German quilts. With her husband, Richard, she has amassed a collection of over 130 Missouri and Illinois quilts.

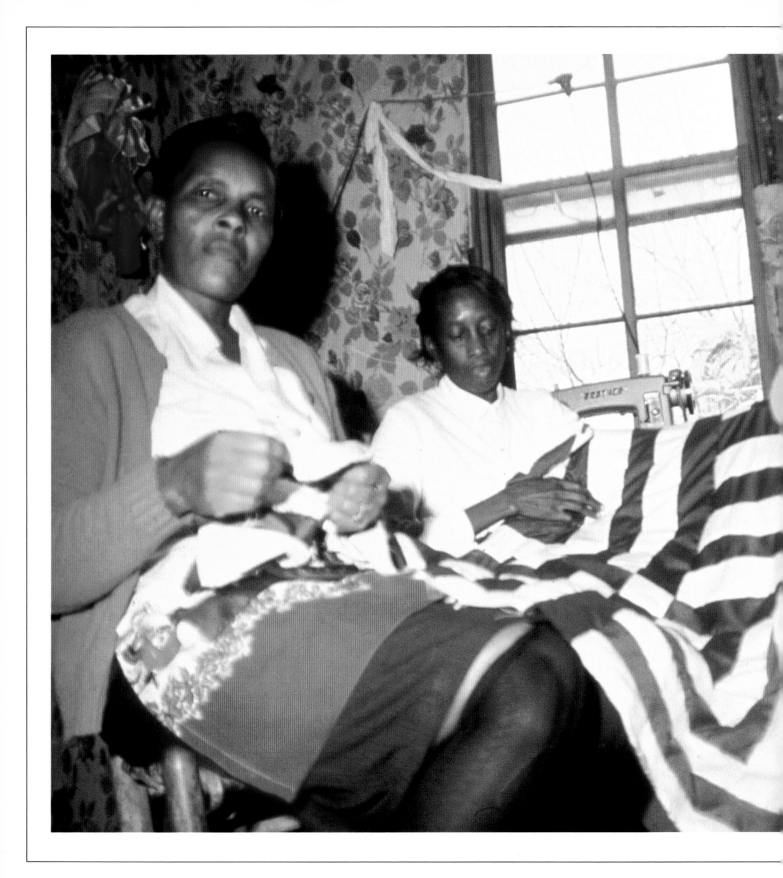

"Helping the Peoples to Help Themselves"

By Nancy Callahan

WE *was catching hell down here before Martin Luther King come. We didn't have no freedom whatever and we didn't know the first thing to do to get freedom."*

Those are the words of Callie Young, a black woman from Wilcox County, Alabama, who died in March 1982, aged seventy-six. Months before her death, the spunky, outspoken maker of quilts reflected on the conditions of her county before the arrival of Dr. Martin Luther King, Jr.:

"It's sad for me to think of what we went through with. Treated like a dog, and us a human just like the white peoples was. We couldn't even vote for our rights. We couldn't walk up in the store or meet you on the street and talk with you. I ain't talking about a white *man*. They wasn't even speaking to us till Martin Luther King come here. What if I was lost on a street? I would be scared to ask you to show me which way to go."

A field hand since childhood who worked on land tracts owned by whites, Callie Young went to school about four months a year. Because public education was not available to blacks when she was growing up in Wilcox County, she walked three miles to private, make-do classes for black children. Some parents paid forty or fifty cents a month for their children's tuition; when they were unable to pay, the youngsters were sent back home. Callie Young's family kept her in school by giving the teachers sweet potatoes, sorghum, meal and meat. After she completed the sixth grade, she went to work full-time in the

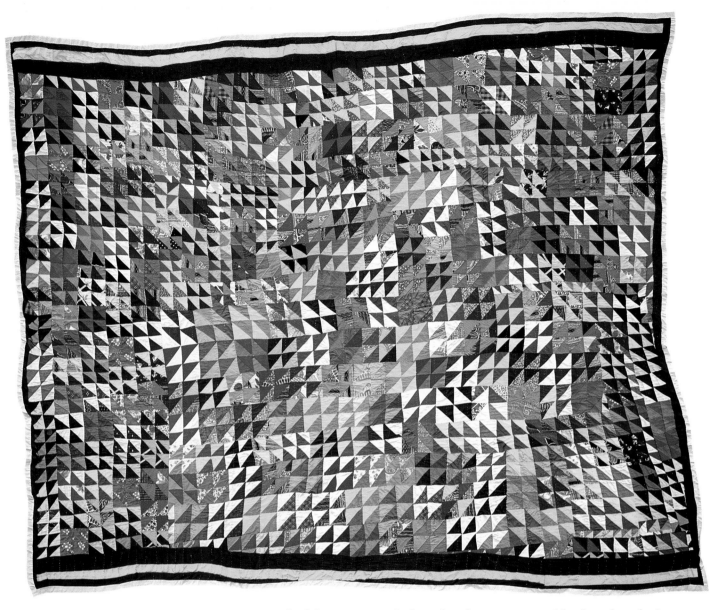

Four Patch *variation, by Mattie Ross, Gee's Bend, Alabama, 97 × 79 inches, pieced cottons, cotton blends and synthetics.*
Collection of the quiltmaker.

fields, picking cotton, chopping corn stalks and cutting bushes. "I wouldn't like to live that life over again. Sometimes we couldn't get clothes to wear, food to eat. It wasn't bright at all."

On Mrs. Young's piece of the planet, the black population outnumbered the whites by more than three to one; but, since shortly after 1800 when this south-central Alabama county had been settled, the racially segregated way of life was dictated by the whites in their own best interest.

IN the spring of 1965, when Callie Young was almost sixty, she and many of her black neighbors from this century-old agricultural community traveled forty miles or more up to Selma, to march with Dr. King to the state capitol at Montgomery. Many of her quilting friends were in that number, including her down-the-road neighbor, Estelle Witherspoon. Their march was soon regarded as a bench mark in the national campaign to protest the denial of black voting rights.

For almost half of 1965, the Black Belt, this multi-countied section of dark, fertile soil in the Selma area, was the center of national attention. Voting rights came on August 6, and local blacks registered en masse but, by December, life for the black people of Wilcox County took on a new form of cruelty. By the dozens, they were being evicted from their rental shacks or facing bank-loan foreclosures on their home mortgages for having registered or having been seen in demon-

strations. Stores stopped credit to movement workers. Jobs were lost. Loan applications were delayed. Tenant farmers with years of good credit were asked to pay up in less than two weeks. With little money, poor education, few jobs and inadequate housing, blacks were now threatened with being driven from the only community they had known.

Some weeks earlier, a thirty-three-year-old white Episcopal priest, born in Mobile, had come home to work against racism in Alabama after having served a New Jersey ghetto congregation. He had been appointed executive director of the new Selma Inter-religious Project, composed of several church and synagogue groups who had marched with Dr. King and wanted to keep alive the spirit of Selma-to-Montgomery.

Soon after his arrival, Father Francis X. Walter centered his attention on the troubles in Wilcox. He documented cases of white harassment against blacks in the movement and sent his evidence to the FBI, mistakenly believing that federal agency would prosecute the guilty whites, utilizing the newly enacted civil rights legislation.

On December 9, 1965, Father Walter was driving through the hamlet of Possum Bend, which skirts the Alabama River. Dead-ended at a bank in the water, the civil rights worker was looking to find his way when he noticed a clothesline outside a nearby cabin: on it were three quilts. He was caught by their bold, inventive designs and by the strength of their geometry, and he instantly realized that the selling of patchwork quilts could increase pride

▲ Fence Rail *(called "Strap" by the maker), by Mattie Ross, Gee's Bend, Alabama, pieced cottons and cotton blends. Collection of the quiltmaker.*

Crazy, *by Minsie Lee Pettway, Gee's ▶ Bend, Alabama, c. 1967, pieced wools. Collection of Mr. and Mrs. Charles J. McCarthy.*

and participation among local black women in the civil rights movement. These quilts were unlike any he had ever seen, because his knowledge of quilts was limited to the styles made by white needlewomen.

With him that day was a white seminary student from the North who had come to the Black Belt to work in the civil rights movement. The two men left their car and walked toward the cabin far away from the road.

"After opening a gate and going through, I saw a woman who looked as though she had urgent business in the back-property wood lot," Father Walter remembers. "I yelled and she just went on about her business, so when I got halfway up to the house, there wasn't anybody there." He would be told later that, upon seeing the two white men, Ora McDaniels had fled to the fields to hide.

Three weeks later, Father Walter returned with a black woman

from Camden who worked in the civil rights movement. "Mrs. McDaniels said she had run into the woods; a white man was coming to see her and she didn't know him. She was afraid, so she had run away. She knew my black associate, so it was okay for us to sit down and talk. I asked her if she would be interested in selling some quilts."

It was hardly an idle proposition. Father Walter and his black co-worker had stopped by the home of another Wilcox black woman to talk quilts soon after his failed attempt to meet Mrs. McDaniels. He had learned that

THEODORE KLITZKE

Two early quilts by members, photographed at Freedom's exhibition in Camden, Alabama, August 1966.

the woman's compensation was five dollars for three quilts, with the white buyer supplying scraps and thread. Since then, he had shared the story with a friend, Tom Screven, a white Alabamian who was working in New York City as a representative for a wholesale carpet company. Screven offered to organize a quilt auction in New York if Father Walter would acquire a sufficient number and ship them. The priest agreed, then began going door to door in search of saleable handworks.

The task was an easy one, for he found a potent black culture with many active quiltmakers. Based on a steadfast faith in God, it was a homogeneous network with visiting in homes, community care for the sick, community burial of the dead, weddings, church suppers, choir contests, singers who traveled from one church to another, story tellings — and quilting circles.

One member of such a circle was Mattie Ross who, at eighty-

four, still sings in the Pleasant Grove Baptist Church choir. Many of her personal quilts had been completed with help from the other women of her choir. " I was always with the choir members," she explains, " 'cause the choir members would be together quilting. We had a lot of fun around the quilts, sometimes cooking and eating, too."

As many as twelve women would convene in Mrs. Ross's home to quilt. After an entire day, they would go home to cook supper and return for the evening. For refreshment she would serve peanuts and sweet potatoes. " I had plenty of sweet potatoes. Go that quilt and eat a sweet potato. We would sing and we would shout!"

Father Walter borrowed seven hundred dollars from a civil rights fund to buy seventy quilts for ten dollars each, and he shipped them off to Screven for his New York auction. Ten dollars was more than any of the women had ever received for a quilt, and for many

it was equivalent to a week's income. "So if this crazy white man never showed up again," recalls Father Walter, "it really didn't matter. But my goodness, if he actually was going to do what he said, rather unheard of for white people, that would be even better. What was there to lose?"

Some of the quilts were made especially for New York. Others were taken off beds. Still others were pulled from storage hampers, neaty folded family treasures sold for the need of a ten-dollar bill. Among the eye-catchers were those with strong splotches of black in the multi-colored motifs or all-black designs dominating white backgrounds. And there were many two-toned quilts in other colors.

As Father Walter went from door to door, collecting quilts, Tom Screven was busily promoting the New York City auction. With limited personal funds, Screven showed samples of the quilts and gained the free services of civil rights sympathizers: a photographer donated the use of his large studio for the auction; a motion-picture publicist who had grown up in Birmingham wrote promotional items; several fabric houses donated cloth samples which he shipped to Wilcox County.

"I figured at some point I had sent two thousand pounds of fabric down there," says Screven. "I sent them Railway Express because it was the cheapest way. I scrounged up money for the shipping from friends, because I wasn't making a lot."

In the midst of it all, enthusiasm among the women for a quilting co-operative developed. Co-operatives were not new to the

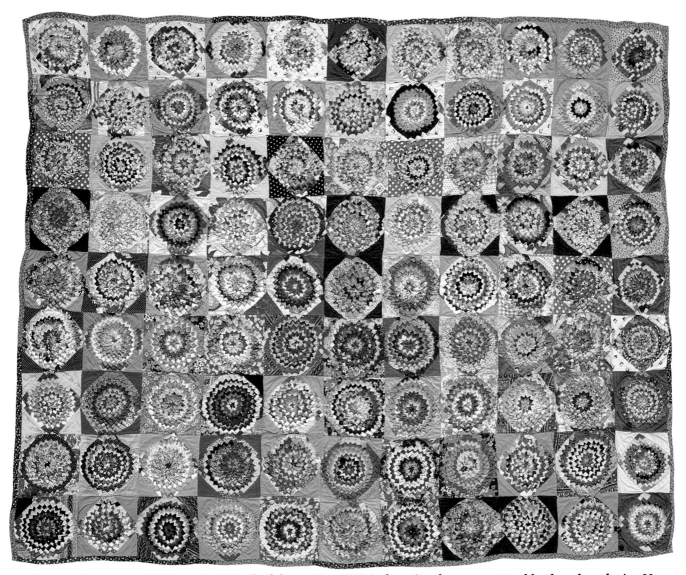

Pine Burr, by Lucy Marie Mingo, Gee's Bend, Alabama, 84 × 69½ inches, pieced cottons, cotton blends and synthetics. Mrs. Mingo's aunt by marriage, China Grove Myles, developed the elaborate piecing technique employed in the Pine Burr design. Collection of the quiltmaker.

people of Wilcox County, the site of a federal farming co-operative from 1937 to 1945. On March 26, 1966, more than sixty quilters met at a church in Camden and legally established their own co-operative, the Freedom Quilting Bee.

On the next evening, Screven's auction was held in New York City. Up for bid that night were patchwork quilts of flour, fertilizer and sugar sacks, castoff shirts and dresses, and sample swatches from the finest fabrics available in New York. Only forty people came to this first auction, but forty-two quilts sold at an average price of twenty-seven dollars—a good price in 1966 for a patchwork quilt. More than eleven hundred dollars was channeled through the new Freedom Quilting Bee to an appreciative group of quiltmakers.

This small success emboldened Screven. With old and new volunteers and new Black Belt shipments, he staged another auction on May 24. More than one hundred people came. The average quilt sold for twenty-eight dollars, and more than two thousand dollars was sent to Alabama to women who, until then, had survived on only a few hundred dollars a year.

NEWS of the Freedom Quilting Bee traveled widely. Membership swelled from sixty members to 125, while quilts began to sell for fifty dollars, one hundred dollars and more. Quilt orders from civil rights sympathizers came from across the country. Bobby Short, the singer-pianist, bought a black-

and-white *Monkey Wrench.* Folk musician Pete Seeger displayed a faded denim patchwork on his living-room sofa. Writer Edward Albee acquired a Freedom quilt. Artist Lee Krasner bought several. So did Henry Geldzahler of New York's Metropolitan Museum of Art.

The lives of the Freedom quilters changed immeasurably, as did their self-esteem. They realized that their collective could make possible a new standard of living for their families. And, more than that, it could gain economic independence for black women for

NANCY CALLAHAN

Le Moyne Star, by Nettie Young, Alberta, Alabama, c. 1967.
Collection of Mr. and Mrs. Charles J. McCarthy.

the first time ever in Wilcox County.

One original member of the Bee, Luella Pettway, remembers: "I bought a bedroom set when I was working with the quilting bee. If I hadn't been working there, I wouldn't a been able to buy." Mrs. Pettway no longer

works full-time with the Bee because of ill health, but she helped to hold it together during the early days when faith in Freedom's potential was more palpable than weekly salaries. She had been challenged by Dr. King, who had preached at her church. "Sometimes we wasn't getting nothing out of the quilts. Working to get it some day. Many time I'd a worked to the quilting bee when we get a dollar, 'cause I wanted to get something."

Her sister, Aolar Mosely, who lives a few houses away, also worked at the Bee. "I was working for to get paid from up yonder one day," she points upward. "I just love to help peoples. That's all I was doing. I did all I could to help 'em till they got to somewhere." Although her motives were altruistic, she eventually was able to obtain a food freezer, bathroom fixtures and a new wringer

washing machine. The Freedom Quilting Bee enabled its members to buy a full range of possessions, from telephones, electric lights, front porches and indoor bathrooms to medicine, clothes and high-school graduation rings. In fact, income for some rose ten to twenty-five per cent.

One of these was Nettie Pettway Young, whose own father was a slave. Although she went to school for not more than eight months of her life, she used part of her quilt money to send her daughter to college. A farmer and mother of eleven, Mrs. Young once spent three days in the Camden (Wilcox County) jail as punishment for her civil rights activities. "Of course I went to jail," she says emphatically. "I went for a purpose, not only for me but for all those poor, needy peoples, white or black. I had no choice. I was helping the peoples to help themselves."

When the Freedom Quilting Bee came into flower, it was the crowning glory of Nettie Young's life. "It was one of the best things I've ever known that ever come true for the black race. It was just a miracle to me that it happened. And I think all the womens who work here is proud 'cause it have made so much for their home."

If the Freedom Quilting Bee happened because of a miracle, the miracle was that Francis Walter happened to be in Possum Bend on a day when Ora McDaniels was airing her quilts. "He the staff of it all," said Callie Young. "He was a spotless, nice man, and wheresoever he at today, I love Reverend Walter."

Many of the women, including Mattie Ross, believe he was brought by Providence. "The

Star of Bethlehem, *by members of the Freedom Quilting Bee, c. 1969, 88 × 96½ inches, pieced cottons and cotton blends. A quilt typical of the type produced by Freedom in Liberty of London fabrics after Stanley Selengut began marketing the co-operative's quilts. Collection of Robert T. and Helen Cargo.*

Lord just sent him through here with a spirit to try to help the peoples," Mrs. Ross declares convincingly. "He was a good-hearted man who had a heart for poor peoples."

BEFORE the end of 1966, the Freedom Quilting Bee was part of a national rebirth of interest in patchwork. First, the quilters made a contract with Parish-Hadley, the New York interior design firm. Mrs. Parish had decorated the White House for Jacqueline Kennedy. Now she

was sending orders to the Black Belt for quilted material to decorate the homes of such clients as Babe Paley, wife of the board chairman of CBS. Mrs. Parish believed the best way to make the Wilcox quilts fashionable was to feature Freedom quilts in major national magazines. One of her friends was Diana Vreeland, editor of *Vogue*, who began promoting the quilters in her magazine. The Parish-Vreeland-Freedom concert was magic. It helped launch a new look in the nation's interior decor; this meant that,

through the end of the 1960's, the Bee received orders from New York's Bloomingdale's, Saks Fifth Avenue and Lord and Taylor.

By 1968, Freedom's leaders realized that, if their co-operative were to survive commercially, some changes had to be made. They could not succeed unless a customer in Bloomingdale's could order a Freedom quilt just like the one on display, and get one *just* like the one on display. If a customer bought a quilt guaranteed not to change colors when it was washed, the quilt had to be

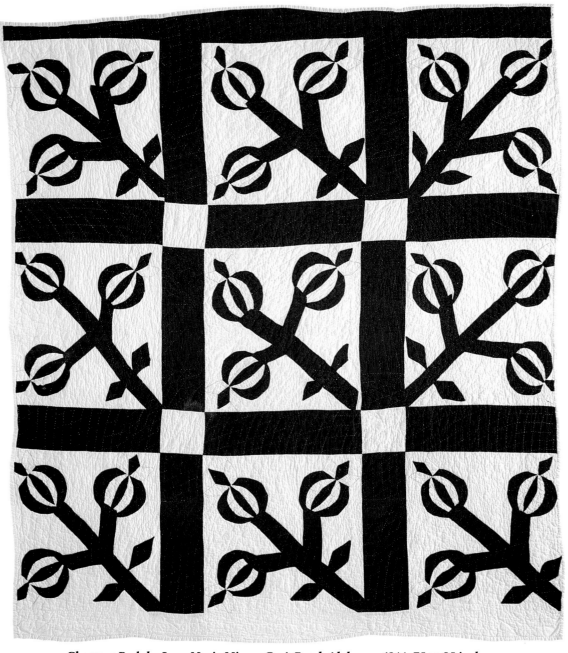

**Chestnut Bud, *by Lucy Marie Mingo, Gee's Bend, Alabama, 1966, 75 × 85 inches,
pieced and appliquéd cottons. Collection of Diana Vreeland.***

made with materials that would not run. If a customer paid for a queen-size quilt, she did not want one three inches too short.

So Stanley Selengut, a New York entrepreneur who had introduced to the world the Andean ski mask, was brought in to change the very character of the Freedom quilts. The quilts were now made with velvets and Liberty of London paisleys, sewn to a certain stan-

dard and governed by carefully worked-out color schemes. And, though no longer "authentic," they sold.

But the women faced an uphill battle; the Bee did not have a work place. They had been working in small groups in the close confines of their hard-to-warm homes spread across the county.

"Headquarters" was the home of Estelle Witherspoon on a rural

mail route outside of Alberta. With innate leadership instincts, Mrs. Witherspoon first became president of the group, then its manager. She had more education than most of the members, having completed the ninth grade—as far as a member of her race was allowed to go—and having attended the ninth grade repeatedly for three more years. When quilting money enabled her family to move to a better home, her original two-room house, eighty years old, was taken over by the Bee.

Through leadership from Stanley Selengut and financial contributions from foundations, on the site of one of the local cornfields was built, in 1969, the Martin Luther King, Jr. Memorial Sewing Center. It was a testament to the quilters' love for the slain civil rights leader and the cause in which they so actively took part. A color portrait of Dr. King was hung inside, along with pictures of John Kennedy, Robert Kennedy and Abraham Lincoln.

Today, quilts are executed for sale in colorfast, machine-washable polyester, yet there are homes across America where the original, rough-hewn patchworks are deemed priceless treasures: Diana Vreeland sleeps under her black-and-white *Chestnut Bud* every night.

For many, there will always be a twinge of sadness that the artistic merit of the earlier, individual creations has been replaced by standardized commercialism. Yet what really matters is that a group of poor, unschooled granddaughters of slaves, in an economic region that was hopelessly impoverished, could begin to earn enough to qualify for Social Security.

Theirs is the story of women from the fields who believed in themselves and in each other with so much passion that they turned the course of history inside out and succeeded on their own. Theirs is the story of economic survival, of a guarantee that, the next time they are hungry, they will have something to eat.

NANCY CALLAHAN

Estelle Witherspoon, manager of the Freedom Quilting Bee, with quilts made recently by the members.

Not many come to Alberta's Route One unless they live here or are on their way to Gee's Bend, ten miles on down toward the river. When visitors do come, it is usually because of the Quilting Bee. When the telephone rings, the call could be from anywhere in the world.

Some of the women have rollers in their hair. Others wear lush bandannas. The atmosphere is informal. They do their work, sing, drink soft drinks and share secrets. Most of all, they care about each other. It is as though history has melded them into a single soul, the Freedom soul, whose energy permeates the building which is theirs.

Some never thought it would happen, but the Freedom Quilting Bee celebrated its twentieth anniversary on March 26, 1986. Now the priest of a Birmingham church, Father Walter left in 1972, but the quilters remained together.

Mrs. Witherspoon, Freedom's seventy-year-old backbone who has traveled the country to promote her sisters and their cause, is the first to admit survival is

tough. After the civil rights movement peaked in the late 1960's, the Bee ceased to attract sympathizers wanting to buy quilts for "the cause." But, in 1972, Freedom signed a contract with Sears, Roebuck to manufacture corduroy pillow shams. For years now, the Sears work has been Freedom's bread and butter, along with quilt orders from Artisans Cooperative, the Pennsylvania-based handcraft venture on whose board Mrs. Witherspoon once served as chairman. With approximately thirty-five active workers, the Bee also makes quilts for individuals based on five patterns traditional to the area.

Discussing Freedom's future, Mrs. Witherspoon declares, "It's going to take some young people to do it. Some older peoples need to be involved, but it takes a lot of energy to do a thing. If you ain't got energy and a will to do it, you just ain't gon' do it no way.

"We're gonna make it, though. I just feel like we're gonna make it. I got that faith in the Lord and I got the strength and the courage to try to keep on. You can't sit down now, 'cause the Lord ain't gon' step down here and hand you this one in your hand. You gon' have to *get up and go get it.* That's the way I feel about it."

Quilt orders and other mail for the Freedom Quilting Bee should be sent to them at Route 1, Box 72, Alberta, AL 36720. The telephone number is 205/573-2225.

NANCY CALLAHAN is a free-lance writer who lives in Montgomery, Alabama. She grew up in Tuscaloosa, where she received her B.A. and M.A. degrees in journalism from The University of Alabama. She has written *The Freedom Quilting Bee: Black Women Artists in the Heart of Dixie* (The University of Alabama Press, P.O. Box 2877, University, AL 35486).

SHOWCASE

COMPILED BY RODERICK KIRACOFE

SUSAN EINSTEIN

Patriotic, c. 1875–1885, origin unknown, 72 × 72 inches, pieced and appliquéd cottons. Collection of Wells Fargo Bank Corporate Art Collection, Los Angeles.

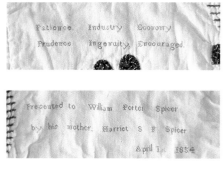

Double Irish Chain, by Harriet Sophia Fyler Spicer, Amboy, New York, 1854, 69 × 74 inches, pieced and appliquéd cottons. Signed, dated and inscribed in embroidery. Exemplary of some blue-and-white quilts, the overall effect is reminiscent of double-weave Jacquard coverlets. Collection of Jean Brady Fox, a great-granddaughter of the quiltmaker. Submitted by the Texas Sesquicentennial Quilt Association, Houston.

The Barns, by Gayle Fraas and Duncan Slade, North Edgecomb, Maine, 1984, 24×24 inches, machine-quilted and hand-painted cotton broadcloth. Collection of the quiltmakers.

Checks #2, by Rebecca Shore, Chicago, Illinois, 1984, 87 × 67½ inches, machine-pieced and hand-quilted cottons, silks, rayons and linens. Collection of Carolyn Jahn and James Kramer.

Sunflower, by Carrie A. Carpenter, Northfield, Vermont, c. 1865, 82×77 inches, appliquéd cottons, padded stems, cut for a poster bed. Private collection. Submitted by the Vermont Quilt Festival, Northfield, Vermont.

KEN BURRIS

Inscription, c. 1900–1920, found in Kentucky, 83½×65 inches, pieced cottons. Collection of Shelly Zegart's Quilts, Louisville, Kentucky.

Chinese Coins, c. 1925–1940, origin unknown, Amish, 72½ × 62 inches, pieced
cottons. Collection of The Fine Arts Museums of San Francisco, Gift of Doug
Tompkins.

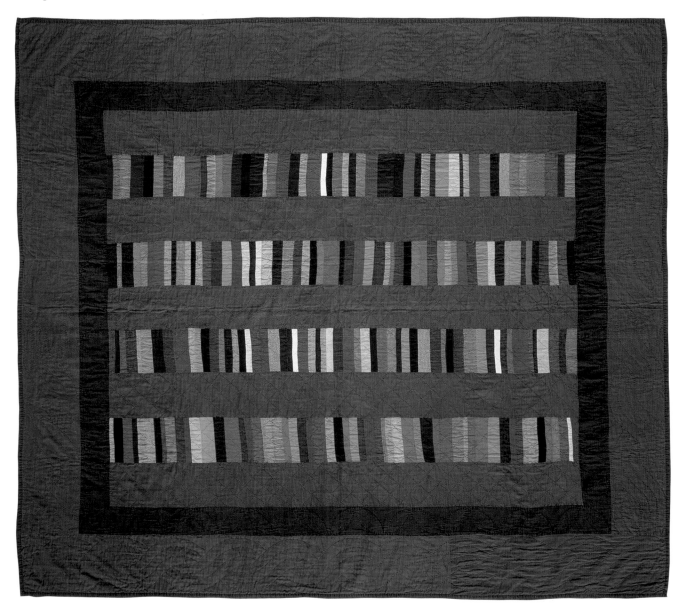

Getting into the Purple, by Wendy Holland, Sydney, Australia, 1984, 82×97½ inches, machine-pieced and hand-quilted cottons, including some 1930's prints. Collection of the quiltmaker.

BRUNO JARRET

Le Chant Hindou, by Soizik Labbens,
Paris, France, 1985, 55 × 55 inches, pieced
by machine and quilted by machine and
hand in cottons and cotton chintz. Signed
and dated in embroidery. Collection of
the quiltmaker.

Friendship, 1848, southeastern Pennsylvania, 95½ × 93 inches, pieced and appliquéd cottons and cotton chintzes. Techniques include reverse appliqué and embroidery. On the quilt are many names and inscriptions, including "Sophia Pyle's quilt piced by her Mother in 1848," which is written on the center block. Collection of Dr. and Mrs. Donald M. Herr.

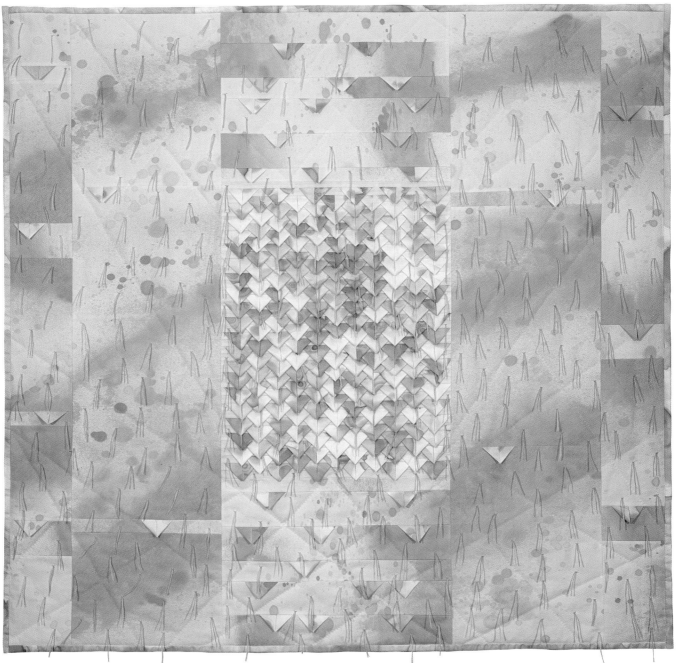

BRAD STANTON

Morning Mist, by Yvonne Porcella, △ Modesto, California, 1984, 50½ × 47 inches, pieced by machine in hand-painted cotton and silk, with "prairie points." Quilted by hand and tied. Collection of Roy Young, President, Fairfield Processing Corporation, Danbury, Connecticut.

Mariner's Compass, by Elizabeth Ann ▷ Darst, Circleville, Ohio, 1840, 101 × 101 inches, pieced cottons. Techniques include trapunto and stipple quilting. Collection of Elizabeth M. Holden, a great-granddaughter of the quiltmaker.

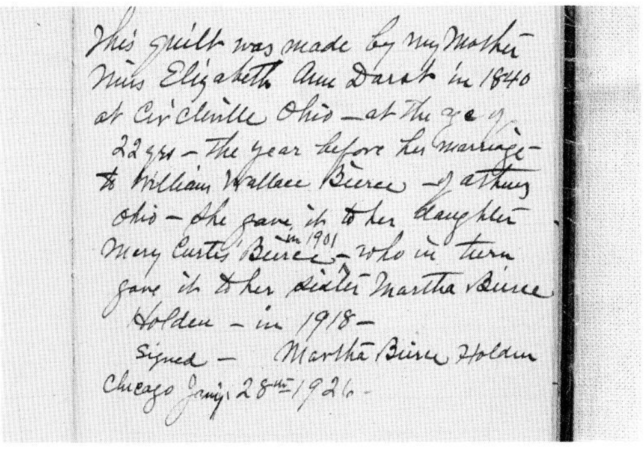

This quilt was made by my Mother
Miss Elizabeth Ann Darst in 1840
at Circleville Ohio – at the age of
22 years – the year before her marriage –
to William Wallace Bierce – of athens
Ohio – She gave it to her daughter
Mary Curtis Bierce – who in turn
gave it to her sister Martha Bierce
Holden – in 1918 –
Signed – Martha Bierce Holden
Chicago Jany 28th 1926 –

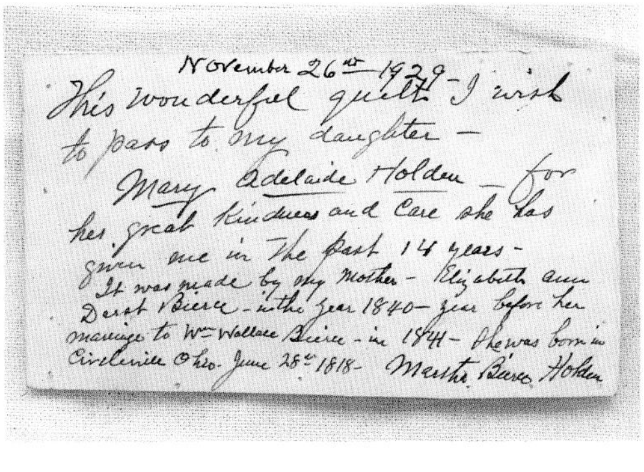

November 26th 1929 – I wish
This wonderful quilt – I wish
to pass to my daughter –
Mary Adelaide Holden – for
her great kindness and care she has
given me in the past 14 years –
It was made by my Mother – Elizabeth ann
Darst Bierce – in the year 1840 – just before her
marriage to Wm Wallace Bierce – in 1841 – She was born in
Circleville Ohio June 28th 1818 – Martha Bierce Holden

Unwinding the M.B.A., by Caryl Bryer Fallert, Oswego, Illinois, 1985, 80×98 inches, pieced and appliquéd by machine in cottons, wools and silks, including clothing belonging to the quiltmaker's husband. Quilted by machine and embellished with buttons and watch faces. Collection of the quiltmaker.

Unknown pattern (often called "Target"), by Lorah Sasser Clark, Grayson County, Texas, c. 1910, 70×78 inches, pieced of "prairie points" in cottons. Collection of Dorris Peeler Saunders, the granddaughter of the quiltmaker. Submitted by the Texas Sesquicentennial Quilt Association, Houston.

Flower Boxes, by Elizabeth A. Busch,
Bangor, Maine, 1984, 33×47 inches,
machine-pieced and hand-appliquéd
painted cottons and cotton blends.
Quilted by hand. Signed and dated in
ink. Collection of the quiltmaker.

44

Molly's Baskets & Bows, by Bonita Siders, Fort Wayne, Indiana, 1985, 84×84 inches, appliquéd cottons and cotton blends. Techniques include padding and embroidery. Embellished with beads. Collection of the quiltmaker.

Central Medallion, c. 1810–1835, England, 114 × 114 inches, pieced and appliquéd cottons and cotton chintzes. Private collection.

The Hot Shop, by Nancy Halpern, Natick, Massachusetts, 1984, 54 × 44 inches, machine-pieced and hand-quilted cottons, cotton blends and rip-stop nylon. Titled, signed and dated in the quilting. Collection of David Cheever.

47

Feathered Star and *Rose Wreath* variation, by Nancy Bogart Hasford, Geneva, New York, c. 1865–1880, 76½ × 87½ inches, pieced and appliquéd cottons. Collection of Jean A. Tracy, a great-great-granddaughter of the quiltmaker. Published in *A Common Thread . . . : Quilts in the Yakima Valley,* a regional quilt documentation by the Yakima Valley Museum and Historical Association, Yakima, Washington.

Nancy Bogart Hasford

Chairs, by Leslie Carabas, Berkeley, California, 1984, 57½ × 52 inches, pieced and quilted by machine in cottons. Collection of the quiltmaker.

Log Cabin: White to Black, © 1984 Pamela Gustavson-Johnson, Kansas City, Missouri, 60 × 60 inches, machine-pieced and hand-quilted cottons. Signed and dated in embroidery. Collection of the quiltmaker.

A Thousand Happinesses, by Laura Crews, Cape Girardeau, Missouri, 1984, 76×76 inches, machine-pieced and hand-appliquéd cotton chintzes. Quilted by hand and stuffed. Signed and dated in embroidery. Collection of the quiltmaker.

A CURIOSITY BEDSPREAD,
MADE OF SEARS ROEBUCK & CO.
GOODS IN 1935.
MADE BY MRS. AVERY BURTON,
DUCK HILL MISS.
AGE 68 YRS.

A Curiosity Bedspread, by Mrs. Avery Burton, Duck Hill, Mississippi, 1935, 74×75 inches, appliquéd cottons and cotton blends. Titled, signed and dated in embroidery. The green ribbon attached near the bottom edge of the quilt is a Merit Award in the 1935 Sears, Roebuck & Company National Make It Yourself Contest. Collection of Shelly Zegart's Quilts, Louisville, Kentucky.

Album, c. 1850–1860, found in Mary-
land, 100×98 inches, appliquéd and
pieced cottons. Collection of Herrup &
Wolfner, New York City. Published in
*Labors of Love: Traditions in American
Textiles & Needlework* by Dr. Judith
Weissman and Wendy Lavitt.

Old Maid

NEW WOMAN

We are to meet once in two weeks and are to present each member with an album bed quilt with all our names on when they are married. Susie Daggett says she is never going to be married, but we must make her a quilt just the same." [1] So wrote Caroline Cowles Richards in her diary on December 13, 1859.

That month, the young women of the First Congregational Church of Canandaigua, New York, formed a society. According to Caroline, "We have great fun and fine suppers." [2] The records of The Young Ladies Sewing Society emphasize a more serious purpose for the group, however: "To cultivate, enrich, and enoble [sic] our intellectual and moral natures, and to form habits of systematic benevolence in harmony with the divine precept 'To do good and to communicate—forget not' is the object contemplated by this organization." [3] Their projects included organizing fairs, holding a festival to benefit the library, furnishing funds for the Home of the Friendless in New York, sending many valuable boxes to needy ministers and families and, during the Civil War, making items of clothing for the Union soldiers. The group met every two weeks, the members taking turns as hostesses

By Shelly Zegart

for the meetings. As it evolved, The Young Ladies Sewing Society (which was also known as The Young Ladies Aid Society) formed the nucleus of its members' social lives and female friendships.

Susan Elizabeth Daggett, born December 9, 1841, was only eighteen years old when she told her friends that she would never marry. But, as agreed, Susie received her promised album bed quilt when she turned thirty. In 1931, at the age of eighty-nine, Susan Elizabeth Daggett died. True to her word, she had never wed. Her choice to remain single was shared by a significant number of the women of her place and time—one in four of her close, personal friends, one in five of her female neighbors.

WITH the possible exception of the post–World War II baby-boom generation, twentieth-century Americans have generally relegated unwed, older women to be pitied as "spinsters" or "old maids." Our century has looked down upon unmarried women as creatures to be mocked, even scorned. Yet mid-nineteenth-century American thought was slightly more humane in its attitudes. Indeed, recent research by women historians has uncovered a startling fact: a substantial number of mid-nineteenth-century American women *chose* to remain single. Like Susie Daggett, they boldly announced their intentions at the time when they would be expected to begin the rituals of dating and courtship.

The reasons for remaining single were mixed. The desire for a greater intellectual life, a dedication to a vocation and the search for autonomy could be fulfilled more easily by an unmarried woman. The internalization of a beau ideal and the inability to find its human embodiment, the fear of binding oneself legally, sexually or intellectually for life to a lesser man, the fear of danger in childbirth and discomfort with the subject of sex were concerns that kept some women from the altar.[4]

And their numbers were large indeed, particularly in New England and pockets of land settled from New England, such as Canandaigua, where Susie and her friends lived. For example, "To the best of our knowledge, the percent of native-born unwed women in Massachusetts was virtually double that of American spinsters in general: 14.6 in Massachusetts as compared to 7.3 percent nationally in the 1830s, 16.9 to 7.7 percent in 1850, 22.6 to 10.9 in 1870."[5]

In both ante-bellum and post–Civil War America, the Northeast

Susan Elizabeth Daggett at thirty-seven, while a member of the Vassar College staff. Photograph courtesy of The New Haven Colony Historical Society. (<Page 54)

First Congregational Church, Canandaigua, where Susie's father served as minister. Photograph courtesy of the Ontario County Historical Society, Canandaigua.

Parsonage, First Congregational Church, Canandaigua, where Susie lived. Photograph courtesy of the Ontario County Historical Society, Canandaigua.

was a prosperous, thriving region when compared with the unsettled West and post-bellum devastated South. Many Northeastern women tended to be better educated and free from the day-to-day struggles of economic survival. And they embraced the moral-reform movements that spread from Protestant New England to the rest of the nation. In this locale, it was only natural that a large number of the young women should question the institution of marriage.

The Cult of Single Blessedness upheld the single life as both a socially and personally valuable state. It offered a positive vision of singlehood rooted in Protestant religion and the concepts of woman's particular nature and special sphere. It promoted singlehood as at least as holy, and perhaps more pure, a state than marriage. As developed from 1810 to 1860, the central tenet of single blessedness noted the transitory nature of "domestic bliss" and encouraged the search for eternal happiness through the adoption of a "higher calling" than marriage.[6]

Susie Daggett was quite likely to be influenced by such thinking. Her father, Dr. Oliver E. Daggett, was the minister of the First Congregational Church of Canandaigua. He and his family had left New England in 1844 and settled in the upstate New York town. Susie's parents nurtured her in an intellectually stimulating home environment. Among the notables of the day invited to speak at the church and visit the parsonage were Henry Ward Beecher and Edward Everett. Dr. Daggett was a very popular minister. "Everything that Dr. Daggett said or did was marked by good taste, and by a cordial and friendly spirit. He was very quick to notice whatever was commendable in others, and was evidently delighted to express his interest and appreciation."[7] And Susie's mother "had a serenity and dignity of manner that were peculiarly beautiful, and, though somewhat naturally

reserved, she impressed all who knew her with her sincerity, and with her real friendliness of spirit."[8]

As can be expected, in this stable, open-minded environment, Susie's education was not neglected. She, with many of her friends who would help form The Young Ladies Sewing Society, attended the Ontario Female Seminary in the town, where religion and the Bible were a major part of the curriculum. Caroline Richards wrote about the beginning of a typical school day:

I got up this morning at quarter before six o'clock. I then read my three chapters in the Bible, and soon after ate my breakfast, which consisted of ham and eggs and buckwheat cakes. I then took a morning walk in the garden and rolled my hoop. I went to school at quarter before 9 o'clock. Miss Clark has us recite a verse of scripture in response to roll call and my text for the morning was the 8th verse of the 6th chapter of Matthew.[9]

The issue of single blessedness was important in its day. Susie Daggett's "Old Maid" quilt is evidence of the conflict of attitudes which surrounded this issue. Although eleven of her forty-three friends in the Society remained, like Susie, single throughout their lives, several inscriptions on Susie's quilt reflect the prevalent contrasting opinions about the state of single blessedness. Similarly, in 1850, the Commonwealth of Massachusetts rejected a bill which would have shipped the state's surplus women to Oregon.[10] And, in 1868, *The Nation* published an article entitled "Why Is Single Life Becoming More General?," identifying it as one of the key social issues of the day.[11]

In fact, single women were their own best advocates. Louisa May Alcott, writing advice to young women in 1868, stated that "the loss of liberty, happiness, and self-respect is poorly repaid by the barren honor of being called 'Mrs.' instead of 'Miss.' "[12] Alcott was joined by a large number of mid-nineteenth-century American women who, like Susie, remained single, entering public life, living lives of dedicated service to their fellow beings, profoundly influencing their era. Among their number were workers for public health, such as Dorothea Dix, Clara Barton, and Emily and Elizabeth Blackwell, moral reformers Mary Grew, Sarah Pugh and Frances Willard, educators Catharine Beecher and Elizabeth Peabody, social workers Cornelia Hancock and Emily Howland, and artists, writers and intellectuals, such as Emily Dickinson, Harriet Hosmer, Frances Bridges and Margaret Fuller.[13]

Yet, as could be expected, there existed a lingering social stigma against singlehood. Alcott's strong words from 1868 are a testimony to the fact that single women felt the need to speak out forthrightly in their own defense.

As more and more young women chose singlehood, they were affected by more than the moral and religious teachings of Protestant belief. Education became available to women. In 1821 the Troy Female Seminary in Troy, New York, became the first institution to grant a high-school education to women, and in 1833 Oberlin College of Ohio became America's first co-educational institution of higher learning. Canandaigua's Ontario Female Seminary, which Susie and her

friends attended, exemplified this liberalization.

In addition, American life was changing dramatically. The eighteenth-century dependence upon family and agriculture was lessening with the advent of

Susan Elizabeth Daggett at approximately eighteen years of age. Photograph courtesy of the Ontario County Historical Society, Canandaigua.

the industrial age. For the first time, women, particularly young women, went to work outside the home, in factories, shops and mills. With modern transportation came mobility and a further disruption of old ways. Many young women, if they chose, could leave their homes and struggle to live more independent lives in cities or towns. Indeed, education coupled with social changes

influenced the way in which [women] thought of themselves, the expectations they held for the future, and the kinds of activities in which they hoped to engage. ...Women began to think of themselves as individuals with their own identities, goals, rights, and callings separate from those of kin, church, or community and defined by personal needs and desires, not the prescriptions of gender. Women began to express the very human desire

to grow, to accomplish, to succeed — they acknowledged ambition, valued independence, and sought autonomy. They wanted to make their own choices, to be responsible for their own achievements and failures, to establish their own priorities and to enact them.[14]

And, although singlehood was foisted upon some young women due to economic circumstance or being left to care for sick or aging relatives, many young women like Susie Daggett made a definitive choice to live their lives a different way. Like Susie, many were well-educated and interested in the development of their own individual characters in concert with the teachings of their churches. Susie, as her future achievements would amply evidence, wanted to lead a life of service and fulfillment and must have considered that a single life could better afford her the opportunity to aid the poor and underprivileged.

In 1848, young Susie had been settled with her family in Canandaigua for four years. In that year, Elizabeth Cady Stanton organized the Seneca Falls Convention, just a few miles from Susie's home. At this time, "Women lost their legal individuality in marriage and became wholly subordinate to their husbands. Wives had no rights to sign contracts, initiate suits, establish credit, inherit property of their own, or claim more than one-third of their husbands' estates. Mothers had no rights to control or custody of their children."[15] In 1855, when Susie and many of her friends were attending the Ontario Female Seminary, Susan B. Anthony, the leader of the women's suffrage movement, came to Canandaigua to speak.

On December 20 of that year, Caroline Richards wrote in her

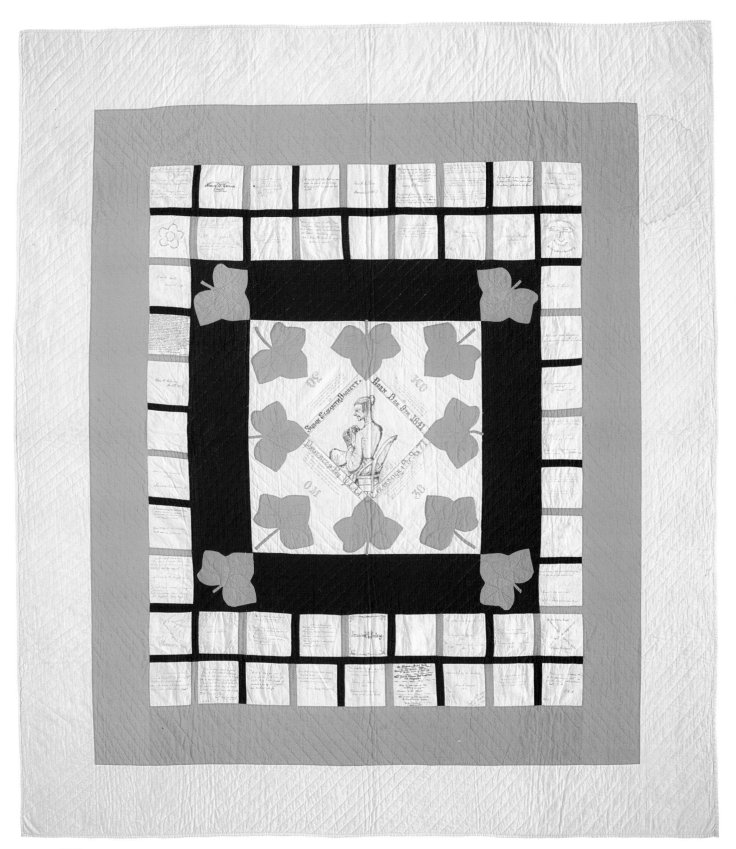

𝒫resentation quilt, by the members of The Young Ladies Sewing (or Aid) Society, Canandaigua, New York, for Susan Elizabeth Daggett, 1871, 68 × 76 inches, pieced and appliquéd cottons. Signed in ink. Collection of the author.

diary: "She [Susan B. Anthony] made a special request that all the seminary girls should come to hear her as well as all the women and girls in town. She had a large audience and she talked very plainly about our rights and how we ought to stand up for them, and said the world would never go right until the women had just as much right to vote and rule as the men. She asked us all to come up and sign our names who would promise to do all in our power to bring about that glad day when equal rights should be the law of the land. A whole lot of us went up and signed the paper."[16] Susie Daggett was fourteen at the time.

The Anthony visit to Canandaigua most likely played a role in her decision: four years later, Susie made the forthright announcement that she would never wed.

IN addition to women's suffrage and rights, other movements were active in the Canandaigua area. Within its precincts, the anti-Masonry movement began, the temperance movement gathered strength and Joseph Smith published his Book of Mormon at nearby Palmyra. Established in 1789 as a county seat, and surrounded by extremely fertile acreage, Canandaigua attracted

farmers and lawyers for the cultivation and speculation of land. In fact, this upstate area was then the breadbasket of the country. Nearby Rochester was even called the Flour City. Due to its wealth, the area was top-heavy with professional classes. This helped to stimulate the founding of numerous secondary academies and colleges, like the Ontario Female Seminary.

Early settlers, mostly from New England, flocked to the area,

Main Street, Canandaigua, New York, 1872. Photograph courtesy of the Ontario County Historical Society, Canandaigua.

bringing their wealth, customs and traditions with them. Good roads, the railroads and the proximity of the Erie Canal gave Canandaigua access to people and ideas. It had such a reputation for being a scenic area that it was part of the tour for European travelers headed for Niagara Falls. This combination of accessibility, early development, a strong economy and a large professional class committed to education fostered an atmosphere that was receptive to new ideas.

Many visitors, like Susan B. Anthony, came to share their ideas and experiences with its citizens. And male friends of The Young Ladies Sewing Society's members went off to attend Yale, Williams and Princeton. Exotic gifts were sent from faraway places. Caroline Richards' father, for example, once sent a box of dates, figs, oranges and pomegranates from New Orleans. Abby Clark, a member of the Society, took pride in her father's election as Governor of New York in 1854, and a neighbor was Francis Granger, the United States Postmaster. At age eleven, the girls read *Gulliver's Travels* and took music lessons. As teenagers, many traveled to New York City on a regular basis and knew the latest fashions, fads and styles. It is in this sort of atmosphere that Susie and her friends grew to maturity.

As she reached an important time in any young woman's life, leaving her teenage years, the Civil War began and took her attention from more personal interests. Susie and her friends were intensely patriotic, filled with abolitionist sentiments. Wrote Caroline Richards, "We have flags on our paper and envelopes, and have all our stationery bordered with red, white and blue. We wear little flag pins for badges and tie our hair with red, white and blue ribbon and have pins and earrings made of the buttons the soldiers gave us. We are going to sew for them in our society and get the garments all cut from the older ladies' society. . . . We are going to write notes and enclose them in the garments to cheer up the soldier boys. It does not seem now as though I could give up any one who belonged to me. The girls in our society say that if any of the members do send a soldier to the war they shall have a flag bed quilt, made by the society, and have the girls' names on the stars." [17]

When Lincoln was assassinated in 1865, Susie was twenty-four. Again, the national issues overrode many personal interests. Caroline expressed the views of her friends when she wrote, "We all wear Lincoln badges now, with pin attached. They are pictures of Lincoln upon a tiny flag, bordered with crape. Susie Daggett has just made herself a flag, six feet by four. It was a lot of work." [18]

True to their abolitionist beliefs, Susie and the society worked on a fair for the benefit of the freedmen of the South. Caroline wrote that the praise for its success should go to Susie, "for it belongs to her." [19]

In 1871, just two years after Wyoming became the first state to give women the vote, Susie Daggett turned thirty. She was living with her parents in New London, Connecticut, where her father had recently been chosen minister of a New England con-

61

gregation, and she received her album bed quilt from her Canandaigua friends. It was the quilt she had been promised years before.

THIS quilt and its inscriptions record love, long-lasting friendships, reverence for the Lord, knowledge of literature and conflicting views on the states of marriage and singlehood. Although enlightened beliefs abounded in communities like Canandaigua, a decision like Susie's to remain single was often

ridiculed. Although much literature of the nineteenth century reflected positive visions of singlehood and single women, derogatory images and negative attitudes were very prevalent. "Popular songs such as 'The Old Maid's Lament,' and 'My Grandmother's Advice' ridiculed the woman who wiled away her courting opportunities and urged women to 'better get married than die an old maid.' "[20]

Aware of such derisions, Susie's friends, some married, some unmarried, planned their quilt for Susie. We are left to guess at their motivations as they picked verses to pen on her quilt. Were they mocking her single status, poking good-natured fun at their determined sister—or both?

Anyone looking at the central figure on the quilt (page 63) who

has not also seen a photograph of Susie Daggett (pages 54 and 58) could be excused for believing the reason for Susie's singlehood was obvious. However, the central figure on the quilt was not meant to represent Susie at all. In a booklet published by the First Congregational Church upon its centennial in June 1899, an essay on the work of the church's young people discusses Susie's quilt:

Any member reaching the age of thirty years, being still unmarried, was to receive a quilt. There is, however, a record of only one member, Miss Daggett, being brave enough to acknowledge the attainment of such great age.... Each member of the society made a block, containing her autograph, but in all probability the central block was the chief cause of this custom being forever abolished. This block, donated by the pastor, Mr. Allen, consisted of a pen-picture of a spinster with her knitting work, her hair done up in a ridiculous little knot. This, by the way, was not intended to be an exact likeness of any member of the society.[21]

One can only imagine the emotions this quilt must have aroused for it to be so thoroughly discussed twenty-eight years later. As we study this quilt today, some of the penned inscriptions seem overly mean. But, since Susie's opinions on singlehood were so well-known among her peers, and shared by at least some of their number, it is unlikely that these inscriptions were meant to mock her. In fact, they may have been sly rebukes of old-maid stereotypes, "in jokes" to a sister who would not only appreciate the double, hidden meanings behind the inscriptions but delight in their creativity. That the quilt survives in such pristine condition is testimony that it was held very dear by its recipient.

AFTER receiving her quilt, Susie remained in New London with her family until 1877. While in New London, according to church minutes, she taught Sunday school and served on a special women's committee created to "render aid and assistance in things temporal and spiritual to sisters of the church."[22] In this work, as in her later work for the New Haven, Connecticut, Woman's Board of Missions, she had chosen a religion-inspired vocation typical of many single women of her time. For, although they sought independence, both physical and intellectual, single women were often dependent upon their families for financial support. This certainly seems to be the case with Susie who, in her mid-thirties, was living at home with her parents. Paid positions were filled by men and the social order of her century did not allow for women to displace men from the work force. Thus, her creativity had to be confined to work that did not compete directly with that of men. She served this church committee from 1875 to 1877. In September 1877, someone else was chosen to fill a vacancy caused by "the removal of Susan E. Daggett from the city."[23]

A photograph of Susie, taken in Poughkeepsie, New York, in 1878, when she was thirty-seven,

shows her at a time when she held the position of Assistant Lady Principal of Vassar College (page 54). Teaching was one of the few professions which women could enter without fear of recriminations from male workers. The concept of a broad public education and the widespread establishment of public schools provided the need for many teachers. Because they were used to caring for young children, and since the pay scale within the profession was low, it was only natural that women would be sought to work in this field. Susie's position was exalted, at least in title. She held it for a short time, until her father's death in 1880.

Then Susie, along with her mother and sister, moved to New Haven, Connecticut, where her father had been born and where

"Like a ring without a finger
Like a bell without a ringer
Like a ship which ne'er is rigged
Or a mine that's never digg'd,
Like a wound without a tent
Or civet box which has no scent;
Just such as these may she be said
That lives, ne'er loves,
                    but dies a maid."

A.B.R.

Susie's paternal grandfather, David Daggett, had graduated from Yale in 1783, gone on to serve in the United States Senate and, in 1826, returned to Yale to serve as Kent Professor of Law. Their return to New Haven may have been forced by finances, and Susie's position at Vassar, though a respected one, probably was not lucrative.

Susie lived at 77 Grove Street from 1882 to 1931. During this period she seems to have dedicated herself to working as a member of the local Woman's Board of Missions, serving for fourteen years as its president. Mission work attracted many single women in the latter half of the nineteenth century. Though badly paid, the women in this movement gained great independence and established leadership positions in the absence of men, who regarded the toil as far too great for the meager financial rewards. Single women, however, whose choice of single blessedness was based upon a belief in a "higher calling," sought out mission work as a way to prove their devotion to a life's work.

At some point during her adult life in New Haven, Susie gave her album bed quilt to Clara Willson Coleman, a friend in Canandaigua, who was among the Society members who created it. The quilt passed to Clara's daughter, Susan Daggett Coleman, Susie's namesake. It found its way through that family to the Canandaigua First Congregational Church's sesquicentennial in 1949.

Susie was reported in excellent health her entire life and fell ill only three weeks prior to her death in 1931. Her obituary appeared in the Saturday, January 10, 1931, edition of *The New York Times,* which mentioned her lifetime of service to church, mission work and education. She is buried near her house, in the Grove Street Cemetery.

At the time of her death, Susie's estate was valued at $100,000, no small sum in 1931. True to her lifetime of beliefs, her bequests included money to the Calhoun Colored School of Calhoun, Lowndes County, Alabama, to Piedmont College in Demorest, Georgia, to the Ecclesiastical Corporation of the First Congregational Church of Canandaigua for relief of the poor of the church and to the New Haven Y.W.C.A. in memory of her sister, Mary, with the stated preference that the income be used for giving the "privilege of classes to poor girls."[24]

Susie's early resolve to remain single did not lead to a sterile, unproductive, ascetic life. Quite the contrary. In her eighty-nine years she led a remarkably productive life whose hallmark was an early decision to remain single, to embrace the Cult of Single Blessedness and to work for the betterment of the less fortunate. A memory of her deeds remains. And so does an album bed quilt, made to commemorate her early decision—a decision that formed the foundation of a lifetime of dedicated work.

That you may be beloved be amiable,

Susan the Matchless!!

—from an inscription on the quilt

REFERENCE LIST

1. Caroline Cowles Richards, *Village Life In America 1852–1872* (Henry Holt & Co., 1913; reprinted Williamstown, Mass.: Corner House Publishers, 1972), p. 114.

2. Richards, p. 114.

3. Records of The Young Ladies Sewing Society of Canandaigua, 1861, unpublished manuscript in the collection of the Ontario County Historical Society, Canandaigua, New York, p. 4.

4. Lee Chambers-Schiller, "Cult of Single Blessedness: Attitudes toward Singlehood in Early Nineteenth Century America" (unpublished colloquium paper presented at The Mary Ingraham Bunting Institute of Radcliffe College, Cambridge, Mass., 24 April 1979), p. 2.

5. Daniel Scott Smith, "Family Limitation, Sexual Control, and Domestic Feminism in Victorian America," in Mary Hartman and Lois W. Banner, eds., *Clio's Consciousness Raised: New Perspectives on the History of Women* (New York: Harper Torchbooks, 1974), p. 121; Yasukichi Yasuba, "Birth Rates of the White Population in the United States, 1800–1860. An Economic Study," *The Johns Hopkins University Studies in Historical and Political Science* 79, no. 2 (1961): table IV-5, p. 109. Cited in Lee Virginia Chambers-Schiller, *Liberty, A Better Husband* (New Haven: Yale University Press, 1984), p. 5.

6. Chambers-Schiller, *Liberty*, p. 18.

7. Samuel Bradlee Doggett, *A History of the Doggett-Daggett Family* (Boston:

Press of Rockwell and Churchill, 1894), pp. 203–204.

8. Doggett, p. 204.

9. Richards, pp. 23–24.

10. Chambers-Schiller, "Cult," p. 20.

11. Volume 6, 5 March 1868, pp. 190–191, quoted in Chambers-Schiller, "Cult," p. 1.

12. Chambers-Schiller, *Liberty*, p. 10.

13. Chambers-Schiller, *Liberty*, pp. 211–212.

14. Chambers-Schiller, *Liberty*, p. 205.

15. Elisabeth Griffith, "Elizabeth Cady Stanton on Marriage and Divorce: Feminist Theory and Domestic Experience," in Mary Kelley, ed., *Woman's Being, Woman's Place: Female Identity and Vocation in American History* (Boston: G. K. Hall & Co., 1979), p. 234.

16. Richards, pp. 49–50.

17. Richards, pp. 131–132.

18. Richards, p. 187.

19. Richards, p. 204.

20. Barbara J. Berg, *The Remembered Gate: Origins of American Feminism, 1800–1860* (New York: Oxford University Press, 1978), p. 91, quoted in Chambers-Schiller, "Cult," p. 5.

21. *100th Anniversary Booklet of the First Congregational Church, Canandaigua, N.Y.*, 11–13 June 1899, p. 64.

22. Church records, Second Congregational Church, New London, Conn., annual meeting, 1 May 1874.

23. Church records, Second Congregational Church, New London, Conn., minutes of meeting, 7 September 1877.

24. From the will of Susan Elizabeth Daggett, dated 21 February 1925, in possession of the New Haven, Conn., Probate Court.

———◆◆———

SHELLY ZEGART is a quilt collector, dealer and historian. She was a Director of The Kentucky Quilt Project, a model for state-wide quilt searches throughout the United States. She is currently at work on a book that will document The Young Ladies Sewing Society and the lives of its forty-four members.

The author wishes to thank Don Muller, Virginia Bartos, Jeanne Martin and Ruth Nightingale of the Ontario County Historical Society, Canandaigua, for their interest, assistance and high standards of professionalism. Special thanks also go to Dorothy West and Amy Zegart. In addition, Dorothy Harkness of the First Congregational Church of Canandaigua, David Park and Lysbeth Andrews-Zike of The New Haven Colony Historical Society, Betty Morrison of the Second Congregational Church of New London, David L. Daggett, The Yale Divinity School Library and The Connecticut Historical Society were extremely helpful in the research of this work.

QUILTS

PENNY McMORRIS

THE decade of the 1970's was a time of change, a time of experimentation in American art as well as lifestyle. But, at the same time, it was a period exemplified by nostalgia for the past. It was during this complex decade that the quilt took its undisputed place as an American cultural icon.

The quilt satisfied the public's craving for both the old and the new: it was, at once, both familiar and modern. It was composed of an ordered, soothing geometry, tactile materials and familiar techniques; it looked reassuringly old-fashioned at a time when we were growing disenchanted with technology and modern-day synthetics. And yet the quilt's often bold graphic design bore a striking resemblance to the hard-edged modern art of the 1960's.

With the re-birth of interest in the quilt during the 1970's, several artists incorporated quilts and quilt motifs into their art works. Earlier, there are isolated examples of quilts made by artists,[1] paintings of quilts[2] and paintings on quilts.[3] But these are exceptions. Generally, it was not until after 1970 that quilts became an important and recurring theme in American art.

Artists made pictures *of* quilts, *with* quilts, and even *on* quilts. They used quilts as metaphors for bygone days and old-fashioned values, and they experimented with fabrics and patterns borrowed from quilts. Had the quilt not existed, it would have been difficult to invent an object more perfectly suited to the times, for it seemed to strike a responsive chord throughout the various segments of the art community. To feminist artists, the quilt was a flag around which to rally. To art collectors and curators, quilts seemed startling precursors of mid-sixties minimal art. And many artists, hungry for more varied visual stimulation than minimal art could offer, "discovered" quilt patterns and colors, adding them to their depleted palettes.

Today, although resistance to change is always persistent, discussing a division between "art" and "quilt" is, at best, academic. Artists are creating quilts, and quiltmakers are making art. Many artists, as evidenced by the works shown here, have been strongly influenced by the quilt on a variety of aesthetic as well as very personal levels. Many have included quilts in works rendered in the more traditionally acceptable media of oil and watercolor. Others have experimented with fabrics, creating quilt-like works of their own, risking condemnation by tradition-bound critics.

It is to this small but ever-growing group of artists, who willingly incorporate the quilt and quilt motifs into their works, that today's quilt artists owe part of the slow, often grudging acceptance of their work by the contemporary art world. Works like those shown here are helping to open the art-world door to contemporary quilt artists.

▽▽▽

REFERENCE LIST

1. Sonia Delaunay made a crib quilt for her son in 1911. Man Ray, better known as a surrealist film maker and photographer, made a quilt of simple squares in 1917.

2. Grandma Moses and Grant Wood have made paintings with quilts in them.

3. Robert Rauschenberg's *Bed* and Ann Wilson's *Moby Dick* were both actually painted on *Log Cabin* quilts in 1955.

PENNY McMORRIS is one of America's best-known and most highly respected quilt historians and commentators. She is the co-author of *The Art Quilt*, published by The Quilt Digest Press, and the author of *Crazy Quilts*. Her work as the producer and host of the ever-popular PBS television series "Quilting" and "Quilting II" is internationally known.

"Quilts in Art" is taken, in part, from *The Art Quilt* by Penny McMorris and Michael Kile, published by The Quilt Digest Press. *The Art Quilt* is the first full-length work that examines, in a comprehensive way, the development of the contemporary art quilt. For more details about *The Art Quilt*, turn to pages 86 and 87.

IN ART

▲▲▲
▲▲▲
▶
Wonderland, by Miriam Schapiro, 1983, 144 x 90 inches, acrylic and fabric on canvas. Photograph courtesy of the artist.

No other mainstream artist has had as sustained and serious an interest in quilts as Miriam Schapiro. Since 1972, her work has concentrated on women, pattern and quilts. A major part of her artistic vocabulary consists of symbols also found on quilts: hearts, fans, houses, flowers and teacups. For years, she has collected bits of old handiwork, incorporating them into her art works. As she borrows from the past, she continually acknowledges her debt to the needleworkers she considers true artists.

As the popularity of quilts has grown over the past decade, Schapiro has repeatedly reminded us that these beautiful objects, so newly appreciated as works of art, are, after all, the work of women. "I feel very strongly that quilts are the great American art," she says, "and that's something . . . we need to be proud of."

DENNIS GRADY

The Dream, by David Bates, 1983, 72 x 90 inches, oil on canvas. Private collection. Photograph courtesy of Charles Cowles Gallery, New York.

David Bates, a Texan who has used quilts in several paintings, combined sampler quilt designs found in books, along with blocks culled from his imagination, to make the quilt in The Dream. *Bates credits his wife with introducing him to quilts, and in his painting she sleeps under the quilt, with a quilt book on the table beside her. He has several of his great-grandmother's quilts, and admires the early quiltmakers' use of "little bits of all . . . different kinds of things. [They] had such a great sense of design."*

68

The Three Fiances, by Robin Lehrer-Roi, 1980, 55 x 46 inches, watercolor and gouache on paper. Photograph courtesy of Barbara Gladstone Gallery, New York.

Robin Lehrer-Roi's painting was inspired by a quilt pictured in Jonathan Holstein's book The Pieced Quilt *(plate 58). She became aware of quilts while in rural North Carolina as part of an artists-in-residence program. She recalls: "The quilts were everywhere—on every bed in every home I was in, on every clothesline, in every country store. I collected them, photographed them...met their makers...and was inspired to paint them."*

While Working on Her Patchwork Quilts, Nana Thought She Had a Vision, But When She Turned Her Head To Look, It Wasn't There, by David Schirm, 1983, 30 x 22 inches, mixed media on paper.

To the artist of the 1970's, the quilter became a kind of folk heroine and, as such, appeared in several paintings. David Schirm's grandmother is the subject of his painting: "My grandmother made her quilts in her bedroom which was so small that the quilting frame formed a low canopy over her bed. . . . When she was ill she would sit in bed like Matisse and sew on the designs. Since she stayed in her room making these quilts . . . there must have been moments of fantasy, memories, and other thoughts to fill the mental space."

Fan Dance, by Barton Beneš, 1981, 38 x 56 inches, mixed media. Photograph courtesy of Kathryn Markel Gallery, New York and Hokin/Kaufman Gallery, Chicago.

In addition to fabric, mixed-media specialist Barton Beneš used such unlikely materials as seashells, canceled checks and currency to create a series of collages based on a Fan *quilt made by his aunt's grandmother. The quilt hung in his studio for a while, and he describes it: "It's such an incredible thing. It sort of 'moves' and I wanted to get that movement going in my work." He tried to capture some of the spirit of the quilt in his* Fan Dance, *but adds, "I didn't copy it exactly, because I couldn't do as good a job as that old lady."*

▶▶▶
▶▶▶
▶▶▶

***Ruth and Cecil Him*, by James Valerio, 1982, 80¼ x 92¼ inches, oil on canvas. Collection of the Shimshak Collection, Berkeley, California. Photograph courtesy of Allan Frumkin Gallery, New York.**

James Valerio's painting deals with the subject of today's quilters, as seen by an artist whose life is shared with a quilter. In a letter about his painting, Valerio writes: "The fact that my wife Pat is a quilter and was president of the Tompkins County Quilters Guild during the time of the painting was inspirational. Seeing so many quilts and listening to quilters talk gave me insights, images and ideas about quilts and quilters.... Ruth is a quilter and her husband is a photographer. Both are friends we met through quilting. In a way I used them as actors to play the part of my association with quilting as I saw it around me—especially the intensity of a quilter and spouse.... The hands that will do the work lay on the stretched cloth to intensify their importance in the upcoming process.... I didn't show a quilting needle in the hands because I preferred the hands clasped to show the union of quilter and spouse and to emphasize more than the act of quilting."

Still Life with Mad Hatter, **by John Stuart Ingle, 1985, 30 x 22½ inches, watercolor on paper. Collection of Amerada Hess Corporation, New York. Photograph courtesy of Tatistcheff & Company, Inc., New York.**

The 1970's saw the publication of hundreds of books on quilts and other folk art, and these sometimes served to inspire artists. John Stuart Ingle's painting (the title comes from the design engraved on the silver cup) uses the quilt top shown on the cover of The Flowering of American Folk Art. *He was attracted by the quilt's naïvety, especially the exotic quality of the elephant and trainer: "Certainly [they] are not exotic in any sense today; we're very used to the circus. But in those days, they would have been the most exotic things in all the world. Martians could have landed and they wouldn't have astonished people more." Ingle uses the quilt to set a mood of earlier, simpler times. He replicates the quilt quite faithfully, making only slight changes, but his painting is not really about the quilt; it is about the feeling the quilt engenders.*

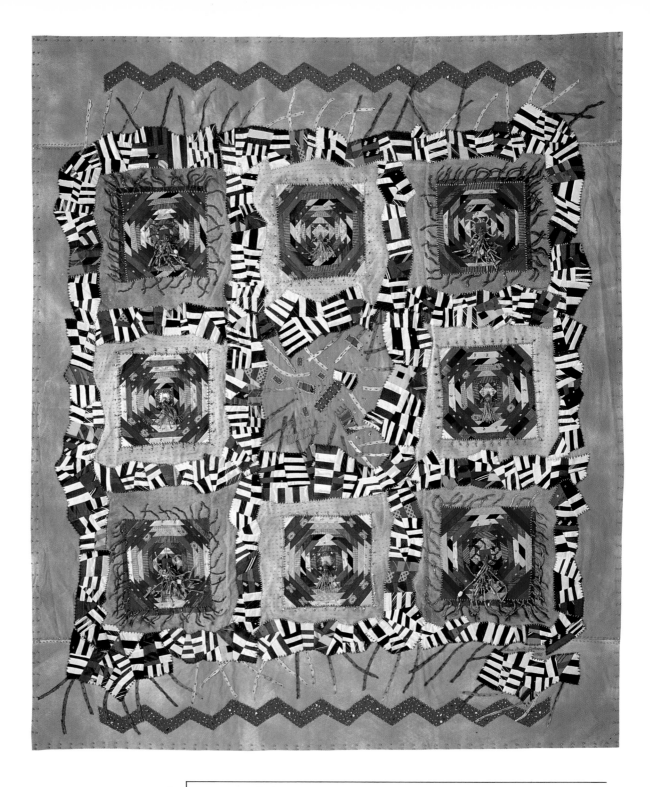

▲▲▲
▲▲▲

***Crazy Quilt for a Half-Breed*, by Jane Burch Cochran, 1985, 80 x 104 inches, pieced and appliquéd fabrics with beads and paint.**

Jane Burch Cochran is a painter, but she has lately been absorbed in working with unusual combinations of fabric which she embellishes. She made the Log Cabin–Pineapple *quilt squares used in this work many years ago from her father's silk ties. It was not until recently that these blocks found a place in this work, which she fantasizes as having been made by a "half-Indian, half-Victorian crazy lady."*

74

▲▲▲

Untitled, **by Jane Kaufman, 1983-1985, 82 x 94 inches, *Crazy* quilt with beads and embroidery. Photograph courtesy of Bernice Steinbaum Gallery, New York.**

Jane Kaufman had been working with beads, feathers and velvet before she attempted a quilt. The quilt developed slowly, as she tells it: "I moved out to the country [from New York] for part of the year and began gardening with the vengeance of a convert. I fell madly in love with my flowers and soon wanted to do 'portraits' of them." She started with scraps of velvet left over from a screen she had made, then set out to do little embroidered images. Her work was skilled; she has done embroidery since she was seven. She had not, however, considered it as a technique for her "fine art" before this project. When the "portraits" were completed, she placed them in a Crazy setting because it allowed her to do more embroidery and because the Crazy asymmetry allowed her more artistic freedom. As she worked, she developed strong feelings about quilts: "Because women have traditionally made quilts, put their 'art' into them, I felt at once connected to my female history — and having labored over one [quilt] as they labored, I became angry at a society that still hasn't accepted this as a 'major' art form."

On the Road

By Michael Kile

Y OU'VE got to admit," my friend poked at the warm Midwestern evening air with his perspiring glass of iced tea, "this quilt dealing is a crazy business. We're all a bunch of malcontents who either couldn't fit into a regular job or didn't even try to. We're nomads, constantly moving, afraid to stop."

Since early morning, my friend and I had been out "picking," jargon among antique dealers for buying merchandise. It had been a hot, humid day, the type you get in the Midwest in July. We had been to a few local dealers' shops, to two auctions and on three "house calls" to local residents in search of quilts in what we hoped were pre-emptive visits ahead of other local dealers and auctioneers. My friend was a picker in the area; he had lived there for years. He knew every back road, the names on all the farm mailboxes and, most importantly, what was carefully stored away in the cedar chests which sat inside the Victorian houses, just beyond the maple-shaded gingerbread porches.

We had not had much luck that day, one quilt and two tops, but my friend had bought a walnut corner cupboard "to make the day worthwhile." For him, it was just another day. For me, it was a chance to get out on the road again, to test my will and determination. Having moved to San Francisco, away from the action back East, I was always anxious to ply my trade on a buying trip. But I also knew that, though I enjoyed "the hunt" and was a

willing captive of its seductive powers, I would never want to work the grueling pace of a quilt picker: I knew, from watching friends who picked every day, that I lacked their persistent intensity.

My friend admitted to sharing this flaw, even though he was regarded as a highly successful picker. As fellow dealers somewhat grudgingly admitted, "He's everywhere." But he said, as he set his empty glass on the grass beside his lawn chair, "I'm no match for Sandy Mitchell."

Nor were any of us. Even in the late 1970's, as my friend and I sat on the lawn behind his house, Sandy was a legend. I remember the first time I met her. It was at a Michigan flea market. Rod Kiracofe and I had just begun to buy quilts together. We knew a few quilt dealers, but all of them lived in Indiana, our common birthplace, and Ohio, our home at the time. Like all beginners, our perceptions were as narrow as our experiences. Meeting Sandy Mitchell in her home state was like a neophyte's first trip would be to that still non-existent national quilt museum: our horizons were immediately broadened.

A large woman, she was dressed very casually in blue jeans and tennis shoes, and her hair was tied back in a ponytail. She was dressed for comfort, indifferent toward first impressions. I remember being struck by her apparent youth, later learning she was five years my senior, and I was somewhat taken aback by her curt, no-nonsense attitude

toward her job. Often, quilt dealers put on airs, mistakenly believing charm will suffice where knowledge is often lacking, but Sandy let us know she wanted to get down to business—a business for which she had experience and interest to spare.

Out of her station wagon, packed to the roof with suitcases, sweaters and jackets, a three-day-old newspaper, books, maps, sandwich wrappers, and bags filled with quilts, she pulled simple Midwestern scrap-bag piecework, the type we'd been buying, but she also showed us an early red-and-green appliqué from one of the eastern states, a pieced quilt from upstate New York composed of early-nineteenth-century fabrics, a Mennonite "eye dazzler" from central Pennsylvania, an album quilt from Maryland and an elaborate *Broken Star* from Illinois. We were stunned by the experience but eager to see more. Meeting Sandy made us realize we had much to learn, and that realization was one factor which led to our ever-deepening involvement with and pursuit of quilts.

*T*o say that Sandy Mitchell has been an important purveyor of antique quilts for nearly twenty years would be an understatement. She is the dealer's dealer. Although virtually unknown outside of the world of dealers and a select group of collectors, more than any other quilt dealer she has influenced fellow entrepreneurs as they have entered the field and, because of her prodigious work schedule, she has bought and sold quilts in such volume that she has literally created buying trends among collectors as the interest in America's quilted bedcoverings has matured.

By her own conservative estimate, she bought over one thousand quilts a year during most of the 1970's. The vast majority of those quilts were sold to fellow dealers who took them back to their customers in cities and small towns as diverse as Houston, Paris, New York City, San Rafael, California, Lancaster, Pennsylvania and, in Rod Kiracofe's and my case, San Francisco. Thus were sparked collecting interests that are manifested today in many of

Star of Bethlehem, c. 1885–1915, Lancaster County, Pennsylvania,
84 × 84 inches, pieced cottons.

the world's major quilt collections. Through her hands have passed many of America's quilted masterpieces as she has traveled the countryside from Illinois to New England, Michigan to Texas, buying and selling, going from picker to dealer, flea market to antique show.

In fact, it is her trips, scheduled back to back, one after another, for which she is best known in the trade. "I'm on the road fifty weeks of every year and have gone through several cars and vans," she admits as she pulls a striking *Star of Bethlehem* (this page) from the stacks of quilts that surround us. Having planned well in advance, she has set this day aside out of her ceaseless journeying to show me quilts from her collection. "I figure we drive sixty thousand miles a year, so we're in the car a lot.

But I don't mind the driving. We're early risers, so we're up and on the road at the beginning of each day." The other members of this traveling retinue are Sandy's mother Sophie and Sandy's Siamese cat. Sophie is a petite, quiet but energetic retired school-teacher who, at her daughter's request, joined the quilt search in 1976. For some of us, Mrs. Mitchell has been the only "mom" in a business populated almost exclusively by people in their twenties, thirties and forties.

Traveling is a big part of any quilt dealer's life. As any successful dealer can attest, if you sit at home or in your shop, waiting for people with quilts to come and call, you will have a very long wait. Most dealers grudgingly put in their hours behind the wheel, hoping that this vehicular game of chance

Sampler, c. 1875–1900, Lancaster County, Pennsylvania,
74¹/₂ × 91 inches, appliquéd cottons.

will produce a few winners. For Sandy, however, the traveling is a way of life. "I enjoy being out, driving, going past the farms, through the towns. For example, I like looking at old houses. If I want to stop and look at a house, or just stop along the road, I do. I enjoy my freedom. I could never be cooped up in a regular job."

Twenty years ago, a regular job meant being a bank teller, then a breeder of Siamese cats. She started dealing in the mid-1960's, but not in quilts. Then, it was paperweights. She started, like most, as a weekend dealer at flea markets and one-day shows. At one such show, someone she knew asked if she ever bought quilts. She said, "No," but soon changed her mind. She began buying quilts for this customer in 1969. "Then, quilts just weren't recognized the way they are today. A typical price was two for fifteen dollars. Furniture dealers used quilts to wrap their chests and cupboards to protect them from scratches and dents." Sandy smiles and shakes her head at their blindness, returning the Lancaster County, Pennsylvania *Star of Bethlehem* to its stack and unfolding an unusual appliqué (this page) from the same area.

A lot of antique dealers thought Sandy Mitchell was crazy. Today, many of these same dealers buy and sell quilts, silently calculating their earlier losses and damning her for her foresight. The more accomplished ones, though, acknowledge that Sandy has worked harder and more intensely at this quilt-dealing business than anyone else in the profession.

Foresight may have been a factor, but dogged determination and an eighteen-hour workday have won Sandy her position among dealers. Driving through the countryside, stopping occasionally to view a Victorian farmhouse, sounds idyllic, but that relaxed scene must be set in context.

A typical quilt dealer's day on the road begins early in the morning. Breakfast, if there is any, is eaten behind the wheel. What follows is a series of appointments, some in homes or shops, others staged in predetermined parking lots as dealers crisscross one another's paths in search of quilts. Lunch is usually forgotten in the course of the day and dinner is often the only meal eaten at a table. Since many local pickers also hold down "regular" jobs, a dealer on the road usually works until eleven or twelve at night, visiting those who aren't available during the day. Then, six hours' sleep in a motel and up again after dawn. String thirty such days together, without a day off, add in three or four antique shows and tote up five thousand miles, and you have a shorthand view of Sandy Mitchell's regular monthly schedule, a schedule she has kept to for fifteen years.

She works so hard, she says, "because I really love it. I enjoy finding quilts and buying them." But selling isn't as much fun for Sandy. "I buy for fun;

Unknown pattern, c. 1885–1915, Georgia, 88 × 66 inches, pieced cottons.

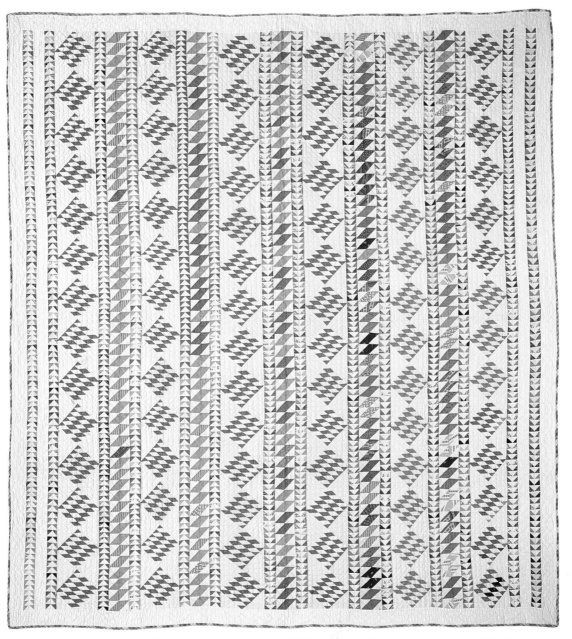

Unknown pattern with Wild Goose Chase stripping, c. 1875–1890, origin unknown, 84 × 92 inches, pieced cottons.

I sell to make a living," she readily admits. But Sandy is constantly selling because "you never know for certain when your next dollar's coming in." Sandy, unlike some dealers whose other incomes allow them to dabble as the mood strikes them, earns her entire living at buying and selling quilts. "There's a lot of stress," she adds. "And it's gotten worse with the years. There used to be plenty of quilts for everyone. Now, there are more dealers and more competition, and fewer quilts available. Ten, fifteen years ago, people wanted to get rid of everything; old things didn't interest them. Now, the tendency is to keep quilts and pass them down in a family." She is quick to add that she thinks, in general, that is a good change, but "it makes my job a lot harder." We refold her Pennsylvania appliqué and open a Georgia country quilt (facing page) together.

Speaking of the increased competition among dealers, Sandy is candid: "It's less fun now. It can get pretty brutal. I wish it was more relaxed." In a business where devious tactics are accepted as in-

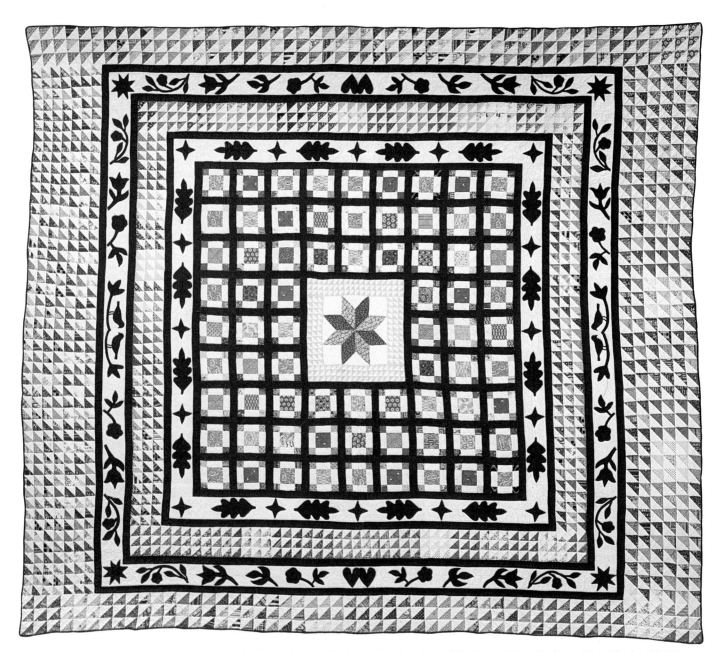

***Central Medallion, by Rachel Vanderheyden, Hudson River Valley, New York, 1848,
98 × 86 inches, pieced and appliquéd cottons. On the back of this quilt,
in ink, is written: "Rachel Vanderheyden No 4 1848."***

evitable, Sandy has a reputation for fair play but adds, "I can be very persistent when I want to buy something," a description her fellow dealers might characterize as understatement.

Quilt dealers often come in pairs, allowing partners to "pick" an opening show more efficiently during its first minutes. To combat the tactic, Sandy devised her own strategy: Sophie helps by staying near Sandy's booth, unloading the tightly packed station wagon, putting quilts out for buyers, while Sandy goes out buying, checking with dealers she's known for years, introducing herself to new ones. "Strangely, as the number of available quilts has declined, the number of dealers has increased. It's as if people picked up a magazine, saw quilts on its cover and decided they could get rich quick by selling them. I get the feeling sometimes that a lot of the newer dealers are in it just for the money. I'm not convinced that they love quilts the way I do. I don't want to be rich. I just want to pay the bills. I love quilts and I love a lot of the people who buy them. It's a way of life for me, not just a business. I'll never have jewels or furs; I'll just have quilts."

AND quilts she does have, as evidenced by the stacks surrounding us. "But I didn't start collecting right away," she admits, showing me her intricately pieced brown calico quilt (page 81), one of my favorites, a quilt she has shown me before. "It was in about 1975 that I decided I was hooked on quilts. And once I started, I've never stopped. I'm a true collector. Period. I don't care what it is. If I decide I like it, I collect it. Quilts, paperweights, Indian baskets, woodcarvings—I've collected all of them. And," she is quick to add, "I've collected them with limited resources. I guess I'm just like my grandfather: I can't throw anything away, so I collect. Once you've collected something, I think you're a collector of it for life. I just bought a wonderful New England paperweight. I'll still buy a great paperweight when I find it.

"I started collecting quilts because I discovered, as a dealer, that I liked sharing them. As a collector, I can lend them to exhibitions and watch people enjoying them. When I started buying and selling quilts, I had no idea how consuming they would become. By 1975, I was a lost cause. Now, I live and breathe quilts. Most of my waking hours are concerned with quilts."

Sandy is constantly lending quilts for exhibitions and shows and she has served as curator for several exhibitions, most notably "Quilts: An American Romance," which is held every year in Michigan. Thousands come to attend lectures and workshops, to buy quilts and to view Sandy's exhibition. Few dealers have shared their knowledge and enthusiasm as willingly as Sandy. She's aware of the risks involved in lending quilts for exhibition (she has recently had a quilt damaged while on loan), but she is convinced the quilts' makers are looking down, watching the activity with pleasure. "I know they'd be happy to see us admiring their quilts." She is also an enthusiast of today's quiltmaking: "There are some wonderful quilts being made today, truly wonderful pieces. A hundred years from now, col-

lectors will have a lot to choose from. The quilting tradition is alive and well."

Having seen tens of thousands of quilts, Sandy, as a dealer-collector, occupies a privileged, though well-earned, position from which to choose a quilt for her collection. Although one might think that her criteria would be complicated, she follows some very simple guidelines: "I buy quilts I like. Graphics and strong, rich colors are my true loves, and I like unusual designs or fine renditions of classic patterns. But condition is equally important. Unless a quilt is very rare, I just won't buy it if it's in bad condition. Every quilt is different, but the ones I collect and truly love are the ones that are unwashed, the ones that have that crisp feeling to them. Give me a quilt that's crisp, that has eye appeal and strong, rich colors, and I'm hooked.

"I love mellow, earth-toned quilts with rich browns, but I also love bright reds and blues." She shows me the blue-and-white central medallion (facing page) she bought herself as a fortieth birthday present. "I seem to have a lot of stars and a lot of red-and-green quilts. I like red-and-green quilts because they are so vibrant and because they are almost always in perfect condition." Putting down her central medallion to show me an unusual red-and-green appliqué (next page), she adds, "I think they must have survived in better condition than most quilts because they're so hard to decorate with. They were made, then stored.

"I remember reading Gail Binney-Winslow's comment in *The Quilt Digest 2* about loving a quilt because of who she bought it from. I'm the same way. Sometimes it's who I bought it from, or where or who I was with at the time, that makes a quilt special to me. I guess it's not just graphics and color, is it? I've owned some quilts three times. I've bought one, sold it, bought it back, sold it to a friend, then taken it back in trade. Sometimes I'll remember a quilt I like and go out and try to buy it back. I can get pretty compulsive about all this," Sandy acknowledges with a laugh.

"I guess I just like all quilts. I've never tried to collect just one kind of quilt, but I also haven't tried to collect every type." She admires early pieces, for example, but has not kept them because she likes other styles better. "The least I've paid for a quilt I've kept is fifty dollars and the most is twenty-five hundred. If you work at it, you can buy a lot of quality within that range. I've always had to be careful; I'm not rich. But I have some very nice quilts. I'm not afraid to pay too much, however. If I love a quilt and feel I need it for the collection, I buy it if I can afford it. It doesn't matter if it seems overpriced, because soon the price will seem reasonable.

"Some people say that quilts are overpriced now. I still think they're a good buy. Sure, fifteen years ago I paid twenty dollars for a quilt but, fifteen years ago, twenty dollars was a lot of money to me. It's relative. People hear me talk about twenty-dollar price tags and sigh; but stop to think what we earned back then. Things are so different now."

Although she's never specialized by buying only one particular type or style of quilt, Sandy recommends that beginning collectors do just that. "If you don't have an unlimited budget—and most of us don't—specialize or weed out lesser quilts and build up your collection's quality," she says, spreading out a rare New England quilt (facing page) for us to inspect. "I think people can get involved in quilt collecting, even today, if they pick a specialty. They've got to decide: 'Do I want to hang my quilts on the wall, put them on my bed or store them away in a blanket chest? Do I like muted colors or bright colors? Appliqués or pieced quilts?' And condition is very important: the price of a quilt should reflect its condition.

"A collection grows as your knowledge grows and develops. As a result, a collection may change, but that's all right. Buy what you want and keep in mind what you want it for. Some people get to a point where they are satisfied with their collections

Rose variation, c. 1860–1880, origin unknown, 86½ × 91 inches, pieced and appliquéd cottons.

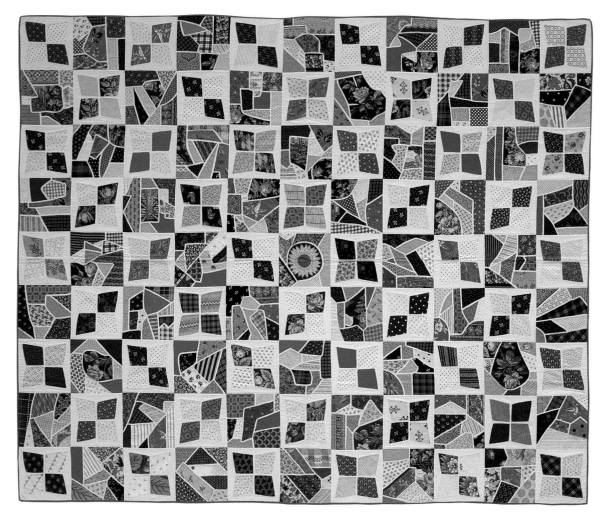

Crazy-style, c. 1875–1900, New England, 84 × 69 inches, appliquéd cottons. Although this quilt appears to be pieced, all patches are actually appliquéd to the ground cloth.

and stop ; some keep buying or trading. I think I'm in the latter category. I keep going because I figure there must be something else out there with my name on it. When you have this collecting disease, you die—*then* you stop collecting!

"I worry about my quilts, about everyone's quilts. If you collect quilts, you are their guardian. Certain quilts *must* be protected. As a dealer, I place certain quilts in collections or with dealers where I know they'll be safe. A lot of collectors are talking now about donating their collections to museums. But which museums? And if you can't give the money to protect and conserve, along with your quilts, maybe the collection should go on the auction block so that someone who wants a quilt, and is forced to pay a competitive price, may think seriously about conserving it for future generations. If they want it bad enough, maybe they'll take care of it. I hope so."

Sandy Mitchell's concern for and love of quilts is at the center of her life. Her dealing in and collecting of quilts is all-consuming. She has spent most of her adult life behind the wheel of her station wagon, accompanied by her mother and cat, crisscrossing the American landscape in a never-ending search for piecework and appliqué. When I ask why she has chosen to spend her life driving the same roads again and again, eating on the run, sleeping in characterless motels night after night, she answers simply, somewhat surprised by my question, "It's my life."

Tomorrow, Sandy will probably drive three hundred miles, eat two tasteless hamburgers and find the motel full when she arrives. The next day, after a few hours' sleep, she'll load up her station wagon and head somewhere else. As Sandy says, "Got to get going. There are still quilts out there."

Other Books *from*

THE
QUILT
DIGEST
PRESS

THE ART QUILT

PENNY McMORRIS
MICHAEL KILE

INTRODUCTION BY JOHN PERREAULT

*T*HE ART QUILT by Penny McMorris and Michael Kile. The creator/ producer of the extremely popular PBS television series "Quilting" and "Quilting II" and author of *Crazy Quilts* joins the editor of *The Quilt Digest* to present the first fully comprehensive book about the contemporary art quilt.

Their thorough examination of the events which led to the emergence of the art quilt extends back to the arts and crafts movement of the late nineteenth century. They recount events during the 1920's and 1930's quilt revival and discuss how the turbulent 1960's influenced the current crafts revival. Their focus encompasses modern art, how it has affected today's quilt artists and how quilts, in turn, have influenced artists working in other media.

Based upon their interpretation of these various influences, McMorris and Kile chronicle the emergence of the contemporary art quilt and its creators, discussing the current state of the art, showing where quilt artists have been and where they might lead in the future.

The authors are joined by the world's leading quilt artists—Pauline Burbidge, Nancy Crow, Deborah Felix, Gayle Fraas and Duncan Slade, Jean Hewes, Michael James, Ruth McDowell, Terrie Hancock Mangat, Therese May, Jan Myers, Yvonne Porcella, Joan Schulze and Pam Studstill—who have spent the last two years creating quilts especially for this milestone book.

These never-before-seen quilts are the centerpiece of this extremely important fine-art volume. One hundred thirty-six pages with 79 color and 8 black-and-white photographs. $21.95 paperback. $29.95 hard cover. $10.00 poster.

The Quilt Digest 1. Seventy-two pages with 52 color and 18 black-and-white photographs. Remarkable quilts, plus Michael James interview, *Log Cabin* quilts, Amish home interiors, a Jewish immigrant's quilt, the Esprit Amish collection, quilt documentation techniques. $12.95.

The Quilt Digest 2. Eighty pages with 60 color photographs and 17 black-and-white photographs and illustrations. Many rare quilts, plus a superb private collection, vintage photos of *Crazy* quilts in a Victorian home, a pioneer wife and her quilt, quilt care and conservation, Hawaiian Flag quilts. $12.95.

The Quilt Digest 3. Eighty-eight pages with 93 color photographs. Dozens of exceptional quilts, plus Quaker quilts, formal Southern quilts from the Charleston (South Carolina) Museum collection, a short story about a wife and husband and their quilt, eccentric quilts, an Alabama pioneer and her quilts. $15.95.

Homage to Amanda by Edwin Binney, 3rd and Gail Binney-Winslow. Ninety-six pages with 71 color photographs. A great quilt collection bountifully illustrates this concise guide to the first two hundred years of American quiltmaking. Published by Roderick Kiracofe/R K Press and distributed exclusively by The Quilt Digest Press. $16.95.

Remember Me: Women & Their Friendship Quilts by Linda Otto Lipsett. One hundred and thirty-six pages with 112 color and 23 black-and-white photographs. A thorough examination of friendship quilts and an intimate portrait of seven nineteenth-century quiltmakers who made them, rendered in astonishing detail. A unique book that will transport you back into an earlier time. $19.95 paperback. $29.95 hard cover.

Our Mailing List

If your name is not on our mailing list and you would like it to be, please write to us. We will be happy to add your name so that you will receive advance information about our forthcoming books.

Ordering Information

Thousands of quilt, antique, book and museum shops around the world carry the books we publish. Check with shops in your area. Or you may order books directly from us.

To order, send us your name, address, city, state and zip code. Tell us which books you wish to order and in what quantity. California residents add 6% sales tax. Finally, to the price of the books you order, add $1.75 for the first book and $1.00 for each additional book to cover postage and handling charges. Enclose your check made payable to *The Quilt Digest Press* and mail it, along with the above information, to Dept. D, 955 Fourteenth Street, San Francisco 94114.

Readers outside North America may have their orders shipped via air mail by including $8.00 for each book ordered. All orders must be accompanied by payment in U.S. dollars drawn on a U.S. bank.

Depending upon the season of the year, allow 4–6 weeks for delivery. Readers outside North America should allow several additional weeks for sea delivery.

We are happy to send gift books directly to recipients.

Wholesale information is available upon request.